Dad,

The family bush

continues to grow.

♡ Laurin + Will

D1194356

THE

NEW YORK CITY NOON PRAYER MEETING

A SIMPLE
PRAYER GATHERING
THAT CHANGED
THE WORLD

TALBOT W. CHAMBERS

NORTH REFORMED PROTESTANT DUTCH CHURCH,
CORNER OF WILLIAM AND FULTON STREETS

THE

NEW YORK CITY NOON PRAYER MEETING

A SIMPLE
PRAYER GATHERING
THAT CHANGED
THE WORLD

TALBOT W. CHAMBERS

ARSENAL PRESS

The New York City Noon Prayer Meeting
Copyright © 2002 by Wagner Publications
Original ISBN: 1-58502-027-3

New ISBN:
978-0-9822653-7-6
0-9822653-7-9

Republished by
Arsenal Press
PO Box 710
Shippensburg, PA 17257
www.arsenalbooks.com

Cover designed by
ImageStudios Creative
Franklin, TN
www.imagestudios.net

Edited and design by
Rebecca Wagner Sytsema

Quantity ordering:
Special discounts are available on quantity purchases. For details, contact the publisher at the address above or by calling 719-278-8422

Printed in the United States of America

PUBLICATION NOTE.

The contents of this publication are taken from a book originally entitled,

The Noon Prayer Meeting
of the North Dutch Church,
Fulton Street, New York:
Its Origin, Character and Progress,
with Some of its Results

written by Talbot W. Chambers and published by the Board of Publication of the Reformed Protestant Dutch Church, New York City. The original publication date is 1858.

While the contents of the original work have been condensed for this publication, the spelling, punctuation, and language have been preserved to the greatest degree possible, and reflect correct English of the period in which the book was first released. While some of the language may be considered sexist by today's standards, we urge readers to take into consideration that this was regarded as proper and inclusive language in the mid-nineteeth century.

Except for the map contained in the Introduction, all illustrations have been reproduced from the original book.

Wagner Publications wishes to thank Tom Mahairas and Ché Ahn for presenting us with the challenge to republish this classic and inspiring work, and Dutch Sheets for contributing the Foreword.

LETTERS OF DRS. DE WITT AND BETHUNE.

AT the request of the Board of Publication, the following Letters in reference to this work, were kindly furnished by two of the most eminent and widely-known Divines in the Reformed Protestant Dutch Church.

LETTER OF REV. DR. DE WITT.

The Volume prepared by my Colleague, the REV. DR. CHAMBERS, entitled "THE NOON PRAYER MEETING," will doubtless attract the interest of the Christian public at large. It traces from the first institution of the Noon Day Prayer Meeting, in September, 1857, its onward progress and widening diffusion, with the blessed results which have followed. It has been carefully prepared, and full reliance may be placed upon the accuracy of its statements. It is hoped that it may be in some degree instrumental, under the Divine blessing, in cherishing and extending the religious influence now spread through our country.

Thomas De Witt

New York, October 25th, 1858.

LETTER OF REV DR. BETHUNE.

The religious public, at home and abroad, must be hungry for full and authentic information respecting the origin and history of "THE NOON PRAYER MEETING," which, as is well known, had its beginning in the Lecture or Consistory Room of the North Dutch Church, Fulton street, New York. This work is the very thing we need. Its author, the REV. DR. CHAMBERS, one of the pastors of the Church on whose premises the Prayer Meeting has been held, has had every opportunity to know and collect the facts. His literary ability will be found to be worthy of his high position, and his deep sympathy with the blessed movement has shed through his pages an ardour of pious earnestness, controlled by a prayerful sobriety, which renders his Narrative both interesting and trustworthy. He deserves, as, doubtless he will receive, the thanks of us all.

Geo. W. Bethune

Minister of the Ref. Dutch Church, on the Heights, Brooklyn.

CONTENTS.

ILLUSTRATIONS.

Foreword.

MUCH HAS BEEN SAID in the context of the recent worldwide prayer movement about redigging the wells of revival. The concept is taken from Genesis 26:18: "Then Isaac dug again the wells of water which had been dug in the days of his father Abraham, for the Philistines had stopped them up after the death of Abraham; and he gave them the same names which his father had given them."

That this was more than a man's search for water is obvious when the entire chapter is read. It was all about a man reconnecting with his past, in order to properly connect with his future.

God was so pleased with this generational reconnecting with Isaac's past, that it prompted one of His rare appearances to a human, during which a promise of great future blessing was made to this early patriarch. Notice that in this appearance, God Himself references Isaac's past while blessing his future: "And the LORD appeared to him the same night and said, 'I am the God of your father Abraham; do not fear, for I am with you. I will bless you, and multiply your descendants, for the sake of My servant Abraham'" (Gen. 26:24). The lesson is clear: *connecting with our God-given past is a part of empowering us for our God-ordained future.*

"Where is the Lord, the God of Elijah?" Elisha asked, while striking the Jordan River with the mantle Elijah had given him moments before (see 2 Kings 2:14). Where did he receive the inspiration for such an audacious act? He had just witnessed his mentor, Elijah, dividing this river in the same manner (see 2 Kings 2:8). "Let's see if the God of yesterday will become the God of today," he was in essence saying. "Perhaps the power I need today will flow out of the well of my yesterday." And it did!

My friend Lou Engle, father of the international "Call" events that gather young people by the hundreds of thousands to fast and pray for revival, actually wrote a book on this subject, titled appropriately, *Digging the Wells of Revival.* The understanding is simply that God wants us to reconnect with the powerful and timeless things He has done in the past, enabling us to build on them rather than always starting over. He not only desires that we be encouraged by remembering His past faithfulness, but also to realize that the promises and anointings released during those seasons are still available today. God's plan is to provide us with a generational momentum that comes through allowing Him to connect yesterday and today. He never intends for us to waste what He has accomplished up to this point in time.

One of the great wells in America's godly past is New York City's Fulton Street Noon Prayer Meetings in 1858, under the leadership of Jeremiah Lanphier. It was remarkable in its scope and influence, touching cities from beyond the

Mississippi River all the way across the Atlantic to England. Only God knows for certain the fullness of its impact, but it is generally accepted that it sparked a revival that touched the entire nation and other parts of the world.

Through this wonderful resurrected firsthand report, you can now drink from this remarkable "well" of the past. The insights it contains will enlighten you, and the stories will inspire you. But equally as important, the timeless anointing of the Holy Spirit upon this well from our past can flow through history to us today, empowering us for a release of the same living water that flowed 150 years ago.

America stands on the threshold of another Great Awakening. We have entered the beginning stage of this revival. What great timing for this "well" to be uncovered! Don't waste a drop. Read it prayerfully and hopefully, agreeing with me that we'll receive a holy visitation and an uncapping of the timeless well of salvation to this parched land called America.

"Where is the Lord, the God of Jeremiah Lanphier?!"

Dutch Sheets
Colorado Springs, Colorado

Introduction.

WHAT IS PRAYER? Prayer is a breath of God returning from where it came. Prayer is the spiritual wireless internet without limitations. No need for a cell phone or computer. Every soul has the software and hardware that can instantly be connected to the living God. "For whosoever shall call on the name of the Lord shall be saved."

My wife, Vicky, and I found this to be true in the psychedelic '60s—before cell phones and the internet. We grew up in New York City and met when we were 16, at the Central Park Zoo in front of the orangutan cage. I was a rock-n-roll musician headed for fame, or so I thought. We sought for the true meaning in life by doing drugs and living as hippies in Greenwich Village. In 1968, we ended up at Word of Life Island through a series of cataclysmic events (friends dying of overdoses, bad L.S.D. trips, time in a mental institution, and shock treatments). When we heard for the first time, "For God so loved the world that He gave His only begotten son, and that whosoever believes in Him should not perish but have everlasting life," we knew this was what we had been searching for. We cried out to God, and He changed our lives forever. Here was a message for everyone regardless of religion, ethnicity, social standing or intellect. God so loved the world—rich and poor, white and black, Arab and Jew—WOW!

This Good News not only transformed our lives, but sharing this Good News with the whole world became our mission. It is what we eat and drink; it is what we breathe day in and day out. It is our mission to tell the world about the love of God, and how he gave his only Son in exchange for us (2 Cor. 5:20-21). What has sustained us as a couple, as parents, and in 30 years of ministry in New York City, has been prayer. Simply calling out to the God of the universe—sharing with Him our burdens, asking Him for wisdom and direction—anytime, anywhere! No static, no call waiting, no operators, and no disconnections!

Since prayer is so vital in our lives, my spirit jumped for joy the first time I held in my hands an original, 1858 copy of this book. It was a firsthand account of what happened at the noonday prayer meetings in New York City in 1857. This prayer meeting is what started the fires of a great revival that prepared men and women for ministry to hundreds of thousands of soldiers during the Civil War. I wanted to know everything! Who started it? How did it happen? On what street did it take place? Could I visit the exact location? As I opened the book and began to read its pages, it was as if I stepped into a time machine with the dial set to September 23, 1857, the Old Dutch Church, Fulton Street, New York City. This location was in the exact vicinity where the World Trade Center recently stood—between West Street and Greenwich, crossing at Fulton.

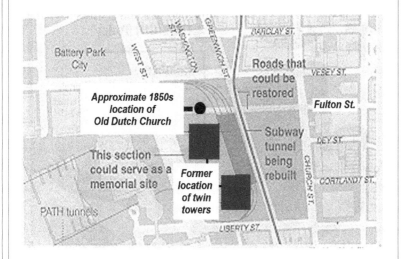

I soon discovered that in 1857, Jeremiah Lanphier was at a crossroads in his life; he was a single, middle-aged businessman without children and family. Choosing significance over success, he began to work with the Old Dutch Church North as a lay missionary. Ministering in the dark slums of Hell's Kitchen, he poured himself into the lives of the poor and needy—people who were homeless, helpless, and hopeless. Month after month he went door-to-door sharing the Good News, distributing tracts, and holding Bible studies with whoever would listen. Eventually he grew tired and discouraged with little or no results. What sustained Jeremiah was the knowledge that he was obedient to Jesus' Great Commission.

Jeremiah would begin the day going from office to office, house to house, and shop to shop; but by midday he was physically, emotionally, and spiritually worn out. He discovered that even as the body needs food, the soul and spirit need prayer. So he went and requested a room at the

Old Dutch Church North, so that he could cry out to God for spiritual strength. September 23, 1857, was the first official noonday prayer meeting. He asked other businessmen to come over their lunch hour and pray. For the first thirty minutes he sat alone praying. Then six men showed up. But God was already there doing His work! Two weeks later there were over 40 people! Soon every church and public meeting hall were filled with noonday prayer meetings. Tens of thousands of New Yorkers were meeting daily for one hour to pray! The result? Over 150,000 new believers! Many joined Jeremiah in reaching the youth and immigrants of Hell's Kitchen.

Finding this book reminded me of Hilkiah the priest who found the Book of the Law of the Lord given by Moses in 2 Chronicles 34:14. It was buried underneath the money. Hilkiah the priest gave the book to Shaphan the scribe, and Shaphan brought the book to the king and read it to him. When the king heard the words of the Law, he tore his clothes. The king knew there was a great need to return and seek God.

This need still remains. This passage from 2 Chronicles 34 shows how God brings about revival in a nation. It is just what Jeremiah did in 1857 in New York City. The cry of 2 Chronicles 7:14 also rings truer than ever, "If my people who are called by My name, will humble themselves and pray, seek my face and turn from their wicked ways, I will hear from heaven and heal their land."

As you read this book, allow God's Spirit to speak to your heart. The great preacher Charles H. Spurgeon put it this way, "He who rushes from his bed to his business without first spending time with God is as foolish as though he had not washed or dressed, and as unwise as one dashing to battle without arms or armor." Call out to Him, realizing that in the name of Jesus you have immediate access to the God and Father of all creation!

On September 11, 2001, as the planes hit the World Trade Center, I was in a prayer meeting in the Empire State Building with the Board of Concerts of Prayer Greater New York. As we evacuated, we immediately felt the need for prayer. We were not alone. From that day until now, not one person has been disrespectful towards God or has refused to pray—from police precincts, to firehouses, from the street, to Ground Zero—men, women, and children continue to cry out to God for help. Does God intend to use this horrific attack to bring revival from the rubble—from the same place He did in 1857?

Tom Mahairas
Founder, Manhattan Bible Church
President, CitiVision, Inc.
www.citivision.org

CHAPTER I.

𝔍𝔫𝔱𝔯𝔬𝔡𝔲𝔠𝔱𝔬𝔯𝔶.

I⊤ WILL BE PERCEIVED at once that this is not a history of the Revival of 1858, nor even of Noon Prayer Meetings in general, but simply an account of the first of those meetings. This first one was remarkable in its character, and still more in its results. For, while there were at the time when it began, manifestations of the special presence of the Holy Spirit of God in various Churches in this city, and doubtless elsewhere also, yet the Consistory building in Fulton street seems to have been the place where commenced the general work of Grace, irrespective of particular denominations—that general work which spread so rapidly over all parts of this country and even crossed the sea to the Old World. But this fact furnishes no reason for claiming any thing for the Reformed Protestant Dutch Church, as though the Revival gave her reason to boast over her sister Churches. Such a thought would be as foolish as sinful. For the Meeting in Fulton street, although held under denominational auspices, was in no proper sense sectarian. From the beginning,

Christians of various names united in it, otherwise it could not have been sustained a single week.

It was a bold and novel undertaking to attempt to establish a Daily Meeting for Prayer at Noon in the very midst of the business portion of this great city; and doubtless under other circumstances, such an attempt would have signally failed. But there was a preparation for it in the public mind made by the providence of God. Instead of coming to an untimely end, as many even of the wise and good feared, it grew and flourished. The Lord gave it favour, and ere long it became the most popular and sought after of all meetings. Spiritual influence radiated out from it. Souls were converted through its instrumentality. Its example was followed in other cities and towns, until a line of Noon Meetings stretched from the sea-board to beyond the Mississippi. The original one still holds on its quiet peaceful way, and at the end of the first year of its existence, is as well supported and as much blessed as at any former period.

Its protracted continuance, and the reports of its proceedings in the public press, have given to it a very great notoriety on both sides of the ocean. An eminent clergyman of this city, recently returned from abroad, informed the author that the Fulton Street Meeting was as well known in England as it is here.

Great pains have been taken to secure rigid accuracy in the statement of facts. Where it seemed desirable, and was at the same time possible, the author has made personal inquiries so as to verify the accounts. Of course, in regard to the statements by the different persons, of facts occurring at a distance from this city, he is responsible only for the correctness of the reports which he gives. But he knows of no reason for doubting, in any case, the correctness of the statements themselves.

THE DUTCH CHURCH IN AMERICA.

"The Reformed Protestant Dutch Church in North America" is accurately described by its title. It is called Dutch because it was originally founded by the emigrants from Holland, who settled the states of New York and New Jersey, and is still for the most part composed of their descendants. It is called Protestant, because it belongs to the number of those Christians, who in the sixteenth century protested in the strongest and most resolute form against the errors and corruptions of Popery. It is further styled Reformed, because, of the two great division into which Protestants were at an early period divided, viz: the Lutherans and the Reformed, it has steadily adhered to the latter.

The doctrinal standards of this Church are six in number. They are the three Ancient Creeds, the Apostles', the Nicene and the Athanasian; the Belgic Confession, published in 1562, the Heidelberg Catechism in 1563, and the Canons of the Synod of Dordrecht, 1618.

THE NORTH DUTCH CHURCH.

This building is, with the exception of St. Paul's Chapel, the only church edifice now used for sacred purposes in New York, which dates back to a period prior to the Revolutionary War.

The corner stone of the church was laid on the 2nd day of July, 1767, by Isaac Roosevelt, an elder of the Church and chairman of the building committee. The edifice was completed within two years at a cost of twelve thousand pounds or thirty thousand dollars.

PRINCIPAL ENTRANCE TO THE NORTH
REFORMED PROTESTANT DUTCH
CHURCH

For sixty or seventy years after its completion, the North Church was crowded with worshippers. Its position, its venerable appearance, the pure Gospel which never failed to resound within its walls, and especially the piety and gifts of the illustrious line of ministers who in turn or in succession occupied its pulpit, all contributed to render it a favourite place of worship, not only with people of Dutch descent, but with many others of very different origin and associations. There was a time not very remote when every seat was occupied at an ordinary service on the Lord's day.

But of late years, the tendency has been quite the other way. The rapid and constant growth of the city demanded ever increasing accommodations for its trade and commerce. Streets once filled with the families of substantial and opulent citizens were invaded by shops and warehouses, and in a short time entire rows of houses, which formerly had served their occupants at once for a place of business and a dwelling, were replaced by stately blocks adapted solely to business purposes. Of course the families which removed to a distance of one or two miles from the church, soon found that however disagreeable it was to change their place of worship, that change was unavoidable, and they must of necessity resort to new temples more convenient to their usual residences. As this process went on, the attendance at the North Church became more and more scanty and irregular, until at length the congregation even on the Lord's day morning was reduced almost to a skeleton.

Yet there was no decrease in the population immediately around the old edifice. But while the numerical proportions continued the same, the character of the people was greatly changed. Instead of the staid, settled families of fixed principles and ordinary habits who once filled the churches there to their utmost capacity, there was now a mixed multitude which might well be compared to the heterogeneous crowd which thronged the streets of Jerusalem on the day of Pentecost. These people came from every part of Europe, and some even from the remoter regions of Asia. The greater part brought with them no habits of reverence or worship, and those who did, very soon lost them amid the breaking up of old associations, and the bustle and excitement of the new and strange scenes into which their removal introduced them. Placards were hung upon the gates of the North Church inviting whosoever would, to enter and worship without money and without price, but very few accepted the invitation.

MISSIONARY LABOURS.

It was evident now that something must be done with a direct view to carry the Gospel to the masses of the down town population. A wide field, especially in the region east of Broadway, lay untouched, and it was white unto the harvest.

This state of things had often been contemplated with

anxious concern by Christians. But the floating character of the population, its exceedingly diverse materials, its devotion to material wants, its want of sympathy with our habits and usages, and its jealousy of intrusion on the part of those in a different social position, all made the work alike difficult and unpromising. Still it was felt that a debt was due to that part of the city and its present inhabitants. The subject was therefore brought before the Consistory of the Collegiate Church (the Church had become popularly known as the Collegiate Church, although that title does not appear upon its records and has no official authority). It was resolved that a Committee of three devise such measures as may seem most conducive to an increased interest in and attendance upon the Divine Word; and that they report to this Consistory at a subsequent meeting.

At the next regular meeting of the Consistory, held June 4, this committee reported a series of resolutions in attempting to make the North Church a centre of religious influence upon the surrounding vicinity. The following resolution was later adopted in Consistory, June 18, 1857:

"Resolved, That the Elders and Deacons worshiping at the North Church, be a Committee to employ a suitable person or persons to be engaged in visiting the families in the vicinity, and inducing them to attend the services in that church; and also to bring children into the Sabbath school, and to use such other means as may be deemed advisable for extending our Redeemer's Kingdom in that portion of our city; and that a sum not to exceed one thousand dollars be appropriated and placed at the disposal of the said Committee."

The first effort of the Committee was to procure a suitable person to act as a lay missionary. A kind Providence turned their eyes to Jeremiah C. Lanphier, a gentleman who had never before been engaged in such work, but whose character and general deportment led them to suppose that he would prove to be exactly the man for the position. They were not disappointed. Mr. Lanphier has been justly described by the correspondent of an eastern Journal as "tall, with a pleasant face, an affectionate manner, and indomitable energy and perseverance; a good singer, gifted in prayer and exhortation, a welcome guest to any house, shrewd and endowed with much tact, and common sense."

CONSISTORY BUILDING TO THE NORTH REFORMED PROTESTANT DUTCH CHURCH

Discontinuing at once his secular business, he entered upon this work on the first day of July, 1857. The Missionary proceeded systematically in his work. He divided the field into districts, and commenced a course of regular visitation from house to house, calling upon each family, and, as far as possible, upon each individual. When he found them attached

JEREMIAH C. LANPHIER

to, or in the habit of attending other places of worship, no effort was made to lead them away. The whole movement has been free from proselytizing from its commencement. But when, as was the fact in the great majority of cases, no habits of worship existed, Mr. Lanphier courteously invited those whom he met to avail themselves of the large and stately edifice so near at hand. As opportunity served, he offered prayer with these persons, drew them into conversation upon the great and delicate question of the soul's relation to God, and sought by the distribution of Bibles and tracts, by the use of the temperance pledge, and by all other lawful means, to win them to the love and service of the Saviour. The Missionary bestowed special pains upon the hotels and the boarding houses with which that portion of the city abound.

The happy results of these persistent efforts, prosecuted with so much discretion and Christian love, soon appeared in the increased numbers attracted to the Old North. The Sabbath school was replenished with both teachers and scholars, and the regular services of the Lord's day drew together an attentive and gratifying audience. What added to the interest of this state of things was the fact that, contrary to what is usual in ordinary places of worship, the greater part of the congregation was composed of men. Many of these were, of course, transient visitors of the city, but with rare exceptions they conducted themselves as devout and interested worshippers; and the ministers who occupied the pulpit took particular pleasure in preaching the Gospel to an audience of this character.

CHAPTER II.

The Origin, Character, and Progress of the Noon Prayer Meeting.

THE ORIGIN.

THE NEXT STEP IN THESE PROCEEDINGS was one the results of which have resounded through the Christian world, and produced an impression which will never be erased from the minds of the present generation. This was the establishment of a Prayer Meeting for business men, to be held in the middle of the day.

It originated in this way. Although the efforts of the Lay Missionary had been followed by the gratifying results already referred to, yet it is not to be supposed that his duties were always easy, or his best endeavours always successful. On the contrary, he experienced frequent discouragements, and sometimes had his faith sorely tried and his hopes painfully frustrated. But on returning to the room in the Consistory building which he usually occupied, he was accustomed to spread out his sorrows before the Lord, and seek fresh supplies of grace and zeal by communion with Him who is invisible. Nor was he disappointed. Waiting upon the Lord, he renewed his strength; calling upon God, he was answered. His own soul was cheered and refreshed, and he was enabled to set forth upon his daily rounds with a quickened sense of the Divine favour, and a heartier assurance that his labour would not be in vain in the Lord.

This fresh, personal experience of the blessedness and power of prayer suggested to Mr. Lanphier's mind that there might be others, especially those engaged in business, to whom it would be equally pleasant and profitable to retire for a short period from secular engagements and engage in devotional exercises. This seemed more feasible, because it was the custom in many mercantile and manufacturing establishments to allow to their operatives the hour between twelve and one o'clock for rest and refreshment. This period is also appropriated to the same purpose by carmen, porters, and day labourers of every description. It occurred to Mr. Lanphier that if the exercises were confined strictly to the hour, if they were suitably varied by singing and by occasional remarks as the feelings of any brother should prompt him, and if it were understood that no one was compelled or even expected to remain the whole time, but that all were at liberty to come and to go just as their engagements or their inclination led them, that a meeting so free, so popular, so spontaneous as it were, might meet with favour and be a means of good.

Accordingly he consulted with the Committee of the Consistory and others, and although none of these were so sanguine and hopeful of good as himself, they cheerfully acquiesced in the arrangement. No one at that time thought of holding the meeting every day.

Considerable pains were taken to give notice of the intended meeting. Not only did the Missionary in his visits apprize those whom he met, but a neat handbill was prepared, describing the character of the meeting, suggesting the importance of frequent supplication, and concluding with some familiar stanzas on the use of prayer and the proper mode of offering it. This handbill (as seen on the following page) was extensively circulated in hotels, boarding houses, shops, factories, counting rooms, and private dwellings in the vicinity. A placard (as seen here) was hung at the gate-way on the street.

The place appointed for the meeting was the front room in the third story of the Consistory building. At twelve o'clock, on the 23rd day of September, 1857, the door was thrown open, and the Missionary took his seat to await the response to the invitation which had been given. After a half hour's delay, the steps of one person were heard as he mounted the staircase. Presently another appeared and another, until the whole company amounted to six. After the usual services of such a meeting, they dispersed. On the next Wednesday, September 30th, the six increased to twenty, and the subsequent week, October 7th, as many as forty were present. During the interval between the first meeting and the third, Mr. Lanphier had consulted with Mr. Wilkin, the leading member of the Consistory, on the propriety of making the meeting semi-weekly or daily.

HOW OFTEN SHALL I PRAY?

As often as the language of prayer is in my heart; as often as I see my need of help; as often as I feel the power of temptation; as often as I am made sensible of any spiritual declension, or feel the aggression of a worldly, earthly spirit.

In prayer we leave the business of time for that of eternity, and intercourse with man for intercourse with God.

A Day Prayer Meeting is held every WEDNESDAY, from 12 to 1 o'clock, in the Consistory building, in rear of the North Dutch Church, corner of Fulton and William streets, (entrance from Fulton and Ann streets.)

This meeting is intended to give merchants, mechanics, clerks, strangers and business men generally, an opportunity to stop and call upon God amid the daily perplexities incident to their respective avocations. It will continue for one hour; but it is also designed for those who may find it inconvenient to remain more than 5 or 10 minutes, as well as for those who can spare the whole hour. The necessary interruption will be slight, because anticipated; and those who are in haste can often expedite their business engagements by halting to lift up their hearts and voices to the throne of grace " in humble, grateful prayer."

ALL ARE CORDIALLY INVITED TO ATTEND.

Benefits of Prayer.

Prayer is appointed to convey
  The blessings God designs to give:
Long as they live should Christians pray,
  For only while they pray they live.

If pain afflict, or wrongs oppress;
  If cares distract, or fears dismay;
If guilt deject; if sin distress—
  In every case still watch and pray.

'T is prayer supports the soul that's weak;
  Tho' thought be broken, language lame,
Pray, if thou canst or canst not speak;
  But pray with faith in Jesus' name.

Depend on Him, thou canst not fail;
  Make all thy wants and wishes known;
Fear not, His merits must prevail;
  Ask but in faith—it shall be done.

How to Pray Aright.

I often say my prayers—
  But do I ever pray?
Or do the wishes of my heart
  Suggest the words I say?

'T is useless to implore,
  Unless I feel my need,
Unless 't is from a sense of want
  That all my prayers proceed.

I may as well kneel down
  And worship gods of stone,
As offer to the living God
  A prayer of words alone.

For words without the heart
  The Lord will never hear;
Nor will he ever those regard
  Whose prayers are insincere.

Lord! teach me what I want,
  And teach me how to pray;
Nor let me e'er implore thy grace,
  Not feeling what I say.

It seemed to them that there was no good reason why, considering all the circumstances, enough persons should not be found in that part of the city, who would be willing to come together for united prayer and praise every day. They accordingly determined to introduce this change.

The result now clearly showed how wise had been the calculations of him who originated the meeting. The number of attendants, although fluctuating from day to day, yet, when considered at intervals of a few days or a week, was found to be constantly increasing.

THE CHARACTER.

On the eighth day of October, 1857, the place of meeting was transferred to the room below, on the second story of the Consistory building. This is the most agreeable apartment in the whole edifice, and the one which has always been used for regular weekly lectures by the pastors of the Church.

The character of the meeting has been rigidly adhered to; the object of those who had the direction of things being, on the one hand to maintain the freedom and latitude of the exercises; and on the other, to guard against disorder, and prevent the single and spiritual character of the assembly from being perverted or lost from sight. A copy of these rules can be found on the following page. Certain directions, or the "rules overhead," referred to in the fourth direction, are contained in a framed placard hung upon the wall (a copy of these can be seen on p. 41).

The "request" mentioned in the 5th direction have reference to communications sent in to the meeting by different persons, desiring the prayers of the assembly for themselves or others. Of these more will be said later.

PLEASE OBSERVE THE FOLLOWING RULES.

BE PROMPT.

COMMENCING PRECISELY AT TWELVE O'CLOCK.

The Leader is not expected to exceed ten minutes in opening the meeting

1st. Open the meeting by reading and singing from three to five verses of a hymn.

2d. Prayer.

3d. Read a portion of the Scripture.

4th. Say the meeting is now open for prayers and exhortations, observing particularly the rules overhead, inviting brethren from abroad to take part in the services.

5th. Read but one or two requests at a time—REQUIRING a prayer to follow—such prayer to have special reference to the same.

6th. In case of any suggestion or proposition by any person, say this is simply a Prayer meeting, and that they are out of order, and call on some brother to pray.

7th. Give out the closing hymn five minutes before one o'clock. Request the Benediction from a Clergyman, if one be present.

The 6th Rule was designed to prevent rash or ill-considered proposals, the adoption, or even consideration of which, would be alien to the design of the meeting and tend to distract the minds of those present.

In relation to the general character of the exercises, there were five distinguishing features:

I. *Spontaneity.* In a few instances, where the leader observes among the audience a person whom he knows or believes to be in possession of interesting information in relation to the work of God in any part of the country, he will call upon the brother to recount the facts to the assembly. But this does not occur often. In general the custom is to let the meeting conduct itself. After the opening, room is afforded to all without exception to take part in such way as their feelings may prompt, whether to offer prayer, to give a word of exhortation, to narrate an interesting incident, to tell of the Lord's doings elsewhere, to prefer a request for the remembrance in prayer of some person or subject, or even to commence the singing of a few verses of some familiar hymn.

On occasion, exhortations have been delivered which had nothing but fervour, and sometimes not even that, to recommend them; and prayers have been offered so ambitious and rhetorical in style and tone as inevitably to make the impression that they were intended rather for the ears of men than for God's. But in general such departures from propriety have been few. To throw the meeting open to all, destroys formality, promotes variety, awakens interest, keeps the attention roused, and ensures, as far as any human means can, a constant flow of life and fervour.

II. *Catholicity.* (Editor's note: The author's use of this word is not related to Catholicism, but is instead defined

as wide-ranging, universal in extent, and pertaining to the
whole Christian body). Although it has been from the beginning under the direction and control of the committee of
the Consistory, yet from the outset has the meeting been of
the most comprehensive kind. Special pains were taken to
divest it of anything of a denominational or partizan cast.
The hymn books used have been those issued by one of the
general benevolent institutions sustained and controlled by
evangelical Christians of every name. The leaders, whether
lay or clerical, have been taken indiscriminately from nearly
every known body of Protestants "holding the Head," from
Baptists, Congregationalists, Friends, Episcopalians, Methodists, Presbyterians of all the various branches, Reformed
Dutch, &c. The assemblies have been composed of equally
various materials. All were invited, and all were welcome.
No man was asked to what regiment he belonged, or from
what country he came. If he fought under the Captain of
Salvation, and spoke the speech of Canaan, it was enough.
There was room for him.

The harmony of believers, so different in their origin,
name, associations, and systems of doctrine, order, and
discipline, was secured by the enforcement of the rule—"No
controverted points discussed." This produced a great enlargement of Christian charity and brotherly love in prayer.
Men were lifted above denominational divisions. Partizan
views and selfish aspirations were absorbed in the overwhelming rush of feeling and desire for the honour of Christ
and the salvation of perishing souls. The progress of the
Lord's cause, no matter in what place, or by what instru-
ments, or by whomsoever announced, was enough to call out
their common sympathies, to occasion hearty thanks to God

for his goodness, and earnest pleadings for the continuance and enlargement of the blessing.

III. A third most noticeable feature in the character of the meeting is the *Presence of Strangers.*

> Brethren are earnestly requested to adhere to the 5 minute rule.

Of course, in a city like New York, the metropolis of the country and the chief seat of the importing trade, connected with the interior by innumerable ties and constantly drawing to itself visitors from every quarter, for purposes of business, travel and amusement, there cannot fail to be a perpetual succession of strangers, and among these, many to whom the value of Jesus is precious. Besides the multitudes who make a longer or shorter stay in hotels and boarding houses, there are far greater numbers who, residing in some place in the surrounding country, at a distance ranging from five to a hundred miles, yet come

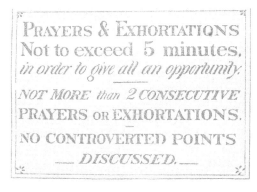

> PRAYERS & EXHORTATIONS Not to exceed 5 minutes, *in order to give all an opportunity.* NOT MORE *than* 2 CONSECUTIVE PRAYERS OR EXHORTATIONS. NO CONTROVERTED POINTS *DISCUSSED.*

into town daily, or at least two or three times a week for secular pursuits. Many of these have made it a habit to resort to the Noon Meeting, as often as circumstances permitted.

THIRD STORY ROOM
IN THE CONSISTORY BUILDING

Scarcely a day passes in which some voice is not lifted which was never heard before in that room. The presence of a stranger is felt as a stimulus and encouragement by those present. Particularly is this the case, when as often occurs, the meeting is informed that the reports, whether verbal or in print, of what God has been pleased to do in the North Dutch Consistory room and similar places in New York, going out through the land, have wrought in some communities like a spark touching a whole train of combustibles. The Lord has seen fit to bless this simple and unostentatious means to the reviving of his people, the awakening of impenitent souls and the general advancement of the Gospel. The echo of their own mercies thus coming back to the point of departure, renews the feeling of former joys, and the reaction is as powerful as it is happy.

IV. A fourth peculiarity of the meeting is its invariable *Promptness* as to time. Precisely at twelve o'clock, the leader takes his seat at the desk and commences the exercises. With equal exactness the meeting is closed when one hour has elapsed. The meeting is exactly adapted to the class for whom it was originally intended—business men. While there is no irreverence, this is a promptness, an earnestness, a directness, which allow no dragging, and show that men have come together for a purpose, and mean, with God's blessing, to accomplish that purpose. The most of the speakers come at once to the point, and put what they have to say into the fewest words possible.

V. We may add to the features already mentioned one more, viz: that which is derived from the one great, original, fundamental object of the meeting—PRAYER.

Its name imports, and every body understands, that this is primarily a Prayer Meeting. But for the felt necessity of Divine influence to be sought and obtained by prayer, the

SECOND STORY ROOM
IN THE CONSISTORY BUILDING

meeting never would have been instituted, or if instituted,
never would have been sustained. All other things are sub-
ordinated to this, as they ought to be. Nor is it found that
this lessens the interest or attractiveness any more than it
does the usefulness of the services. All men cannot speak
to edification, but all men can pray so as to carry their fel-
low-worshippers with them. If only their hearts are warm
with love, if they feel the wants they express, if they speak
as if to a God upon whom they wholly depend, and in whose
promise they entirely believe, no defects of expression or utterance will prevent their supplications from being enlivening
to their brethren as well as acceptable to God.

This is not speculation, but the teaching of experience.
Uniformly the most happy meetings, those which are longest
remembered and are most fruitful of present and future good,
are those in which there has been most prayer offered. This
has been so well understood now that all experienced leaders
make it a point to secure as much speaking to God as possible,
rather than speaking to man; no matter how able, eloquent,
zealous or moving. The life, the glory, the blessedness of the
Noon Prayer Meeting lies in its close adherence to the idea
implied in its name.

THE PROGRESS.
During the closing months of the year 1857, this was slow
but sure. The general interruption of business in consequence of the financial disasters of the season, gave to many
an opportunity of regularly attending the meeting, of which
a more prosperous season would perhaps have deprived
them. Others were drawn by curiosity, and before they were
aware, became interested in the service, and were induced

to attend again and again. But it can scarcely be doubted that the main cause of the general popularity of the meeting was the gracious purpose of the Lord, making use, in His adorable sovereignty, of this means to alleviate the gloom of temporal calamities, and lead the minds of the children of men to higher ends than "The meat that perisheth." In no other way can we account for the eagerness with which multitudes of men would flock together at an unusual, and to many most inconvenient hour, for the purposes of worship, to a place where there were none of the attractions which alone, in ordinary circumstances, move men in masses to attend a religious service. There was no eloquent orator, no noted revivalist, no display of intellectual abilities, native or acquired; nothing to gratify a refined taste, or stimulate a jaded imagination, or cater to itching ears. It was simply a gathering of men who turned aside from secular cares to consecrate an hour to prayer or praise—an assembly in which the chief part was taken by laymen, and these, persons not distinguished for any unusual gifts or culture.

Yet the attraction to this unpretending service became wide-spread and irresistible. Men of all ages, classes and characters attended. Mere lads and men of hoary heads sat side by side on the same benches. Lawyers and physicians, merchants and clerks, bankers and brokers, manufacturers and mechanics, carmen and hod-carriers, butchers and bakers, and porters and messengers, were represented from day to day. They came just as they were from their secular avocations, and entered with zest into the spirit of the occasion.

The other sex began also to feel the common impulse. At first the entire company was made up of men, and the swell of so many male voices singing lustily the songs of Zion was

like the sound of many waters. But after a time ladies began
to drop in one by one, and soon there came to be an average
attendance of about fifty—a portion of the house being set
apart for them—and the singing, with their voices intermin-
gled, became softer and more like the praise of an ordinary
worshiping assembly.

A mournful event which happened at this time added
greatly to the growing seriousness in the community. This
was the unexpected death on the 6th of January, of the Rev.
John Knox, D.D., with two exceptions the oldest settled pastor in the city, and a man universally known and venerated
and beloved. Prostrated by a headlong fall from the rear
piazza of his own residence, the exact cause of which is and
ever will be a mystery,
he lay in unconscious-
ness for some days, and
then his spirit entered
the heavenly rest. The
shock of his sudden de-
parture from full health
and active usefulness to
the silent tomb, affected
the public mind very
deeply, as was shown by
his extraordinary funer-
al—a funeral attended
by such general and
heart-felt demonstra-
tions of grief and respect
as never before had been
paid to the memory of a

JOHN KNOX

man in a private station. He had often, as senior pastor of the Collegiate Church, presided at the Noon Meeting in the Consistory building.

In the month of January, the attendance increased so largely that the room on the ground floor was opened, and a meeting was carried on there, simultaneously with the one on the floor above. By the early part of the following month, the place again became too strait, and the room in the third story, in which the first meeting had been held some six months before, was thrown open to the crowd. This also was immediately filled. It was not uncommon at that time for all the rooms, with the halls and stairways leading to them, to be filled to repletion; these meetings under as many different leaders being carried on at the same time under one roof.

About this time, the daily press of the city had its attention drawn to a topic now become one of universal interest. Reporters were dispatched to the various prayer meetings, and "the Progress of the Revival" became a standing head of intelligence in several widely circulated journals. Remarkable cases of awakening were detailed at length, and all items of religious information were eagerly seized to gratify the presumed demands of readers. No one can doubt that these articles enlisted the attention of many who otherwise might have remained in total ignorance of the work God was doing. Some were induced to attend the meetings, of which they saw from day to day wonderful reports, and to a portion at least of these, the final result was a blessed one.

One immediate consequence of the overflow of attendants upon the North Church meetings was the institution of various others of the same character in different parts of the city, under the auspices of Young Men's Christian Association, or of some older laymen, or of an association of pastors in a single neighborhood. At one time in the early spring, the number of these meetings exceeded twenty, and all were well attended, some being crowded. Still the interest attached to the original place of prayer continued undiminished. Occasionally some poor waif of humanity, some lifelong stranger to serious things would wander in among the worshippers, and be arrested by the truth. The prodigal's return was not only hailed with joy and thanksgiving, but proved a new incitement to zeal in effort and persistency in prayer.

Soon after this, when noon meetings had been instituted and were largely attended in all the principal cities, the custom was introduced of exchanging dispatches with each other by magnetic telegraph. One of these, received from Philadelphia, is inserted as an illustration.

"Philadelphia, Saturday, March 18, 12.15 P.M.
"To Mr. W. Wetmore, Fulton street Meeting:

"Jayne's Hall Daily Prayer Meeting is crowded, upwards of three thousand present; with one mind and heart they glorify our Father in heaven, for the mighty work he is doing in our city and country in the building up of saints and the conversion of sinners. The Lord hath done great things for us, whence joy to us is brought. May he who holds the seven stars in his right hand, and who walks in the midst of the churches, be with you by his Spirit this day.

"Grace, mercy, and peace be with you.
"Geo. H. Stuart, *Chairman of the Meeting*."

A suitable reply was transmitted.

As the warm season came on, and the citizens began to leave town for the usual places of summer resort, the attendance became less numerous, but not less earnest and cordial. Indeed the tokens of the Divine favour had been so clear and abundant that it was felt that the meeting

was no longer an experiment, or a provisional arrangement, but an approved instrument in the Lord's hands of doing good, and little less than a necessity in this great city. Early in the month of May therefore, a placard (as seen above) was hung upon the wall of the second story room.

It is a very remarkable fact that although there was a sensible decline in the numbers of attendants during the warm summer months, yet that it was precisely during this period that the most extraordinary instances of conversion occurred, as will afterwards appear.

We subjoin some notices of the proceeding from time to time. At the meeting of August 4, the Revs. Prof. Gibson and Mr. McClure, delegated from the Presbyterian Synod of Ireland to a corresponding body in America were present, and presented Christian salutations. Prof. Gibson after expressing his pleasure in being present at such a meeting said,

"We have just landed from the Persia; and our first desire was to get into this prayer meeting. We come from the Presbyterian Synod of Ireland, and one of our great objects in coming to this country is to witness for ourselves and gather up the facts of this great revival with which the Lord is blessing you in America.

"We have heard much of this great revival in Ireland. We have connected with our Synod five hundred churches and congregations. And we have a strong desire that the same gracious dispensation which has blessed you here might be bestowed upon all our Churches at home. We desire an interest in all your prayers for a blessing upon the Churches of our land."

The Rev. Mr. McClure, the other delegate, greeted the meeting in the most cordial manner. He said they were not ignorant of what the Lord is doing in this country. He was fully satisfied as were all in his own land that this was the genuine work of the Holy Spirit. "The kingdom of Great Britain has a vital interest in showing this work, and I join in the request most heartily, that you will pray that this work of grace may reach us also, as we trust and hope it will."

The next day when the usual invitation was given to strangers who might be present, to take part in the exercises, a gentleman arose and said,

"I came from India, and I landed but yesterday. I have come all the way from that far distant land to see for myself what the Lord is doing in America. I am an Englishman by birth, but my home is in India. We have heard of the glorious outpouring of the Holy Spirit upon your Churches, and we have rejoiced at it with exceeding joy. We believe as you believe, that we stand in the first breaking light of a most eventful day—an era of greater displays of Divine grace in the salvation of sinners than the world has ever seen. We need faith that is equal to the times. We need confidence to ask great things of God, and we shall get great things. Ask little things, and we shall get little things. But ask mighty showers of grace, and they will be poured out like a flood upon us."

Here we conclude the account of the Progress of the Meeting. At the time this volume is sent to the press, the two rooms on the first and second floors of the Consistory building are still from day to day well filled and sometimes crowded. Strangers and citizens resort to the well known place. Earnest Christians find it a sort of second home, and awakened sinners gravitate thither by a kind of natural law, as to the place where in the interval of services in their own churches, they may most surely look for the help and guidance suited to their case. The Lord Grant it may ever continue to be so!

THE MIDDAY PRAYER MEETING.

From the pen of Mrs. Phoebe H. Brown, author of the
favourite hymn, "I love to steal awhile away."

Tune *Ortenville.*

Jesus, this midday hour of prayer
We consecrate to *thee.*
Forgetful of each earthly care,
We would thy glory see.

We come thy presence to implore;
O teach us how to pray!
Impart us to thy Spirit's power,
Thy saving grace display.

Baptize with energy Divine
The contrite soul afresh;
O bow the stubborn will to thine,
And give the heart of flesh.

Unite our hearts, unite our tongues,
In lofty praise to thee,
Accept the tribute of our songs
Thou Holy One in Three.

CHAPTER III.

𝕿𝖍𝖊 𝕲𝖑𝖔𝖇𝖊 𝕳𝖔𝖙𝖊𝖑 𝕸𝖊𝖊𝖙𝖎𝖓𝖌.

ALLUSION HAS BEEN MADE to various meetings for prayer, instituted and maintained after the pattern of the original one, with greater or less constancy and success, in other parts of the city. It does not fall within the design of this work to notice these particularly. But one of them is deserving of especial notice as being a direct branch of the parent meeting, and part of the missionary operations of the North Dutch Church. This is the Globe Hotel Meeting.

The Globe Hotel during the former part of the present year was in the charge of Miss St. J——. She possessed a desire to be useful to the inmates of the Hotel, many of whom greatly needed such efforts. For although she and her house were both most respectable, yet as a cheap lodging house open to all who behaved orderly while in it, it contained many of those who in the old world are called "the dangerous classes," and here are usually the neglected classes.

The proprietress refused to let her bar room for the liquor business, although offered $800 a year for the privilege. At the suggestion of Mr. Lanphier, she fitted up the room very comfortably, and opened it every Thursday evening for a free Prayer Meeting, designed for the residents in that vicinity, who were told that now they had a meeting just at their doors, and one which they might attend in their plainest and most ordinary clothing. The meetings were commenced on the 1st day of July. Subsequent meetings were held every week until the end of September when the state of her health compelling the excellent lady who controlled the Hotel to relinquish the business, the property passed into other hands, and the room was no longer attainable for religious purposes.

But the record of these thirteen weekly meetings is on high. All of them were well attended by the class for whom they were designed. Precious seasons of Divine favour were enjoyed, and many will look back from eternity with grateful joy to the Thursday evening exercises at the *Globe Hotel*. We give in detail three of the interesting displays of Divine grace arising from or connected with this meeting.

THE MAN WHO FOUND CHRIST AT THE LAMP POST.
This deeply interesting case belongs here, because although the man regularly attended the Noon meeting, yet it was one of the evening services at the Globe Hotel which seems to have been the immediate means of leading him to the Saviour.

In the early part of the month of August, a man was seen walking back and forth on the sidewalk, in front of the North Dutch Church, while the Prayer Meeting was going on. He was dressed in the very plainest attire, with a pea-jacket hanging on his arm. His countenance bore the very legible characteristics of a "hard case." After walking for some time, he paused, and coming up the steps to the second story lecture room, said to the lay Missionary at the door, whose daily care it is to see those who come get comfortable seats,

"Will you let such a miserable-looking object as I am have a seat in your Prayer Meeting?"

"Certainly we will," was the reply, "and we are very glad to have you come."

He went in. Daily, for several weeks, he attended the meeting. He had been a man of very intemperate habits. He left off the use of intoxicating drinks at once. He became interested in the subject of religion; and the more he came the more interested he appeared. After four weeks of total abstinence, he signed the temperance pledge and kept it. He grew more neat in dress; his clothing was washed clean, though no man would have given fifty cents for all he had on. He often was without food, having no employment. But Providence seemed to make special provision that he should not suffer with hunger. In several instances he found small packages of meat and bread wrapped in paper as he was walking the streets. In other cases, small sums of money were given him, though never at the Prayer Meeting.

His convictions became more deep and pungent. He had a very sad expression on his face. He was often conversed with—often urged to repentance—often invited to come to Christ. But still he held back. One evening he went to Washington market to lodge. He had been that evening to the prayer meeting at the Globe Hotel, where he had been spoken to on the duty of immediately yielding to the claims of the Lord Jesus. His distress kept all the time increasing. At two o'clock in the morning he betook himself to the streets to see if he could not feel better by walking. His sins lay like a heavy burden on his soul. He could not find the Saviour. He walked and walked, and no relief came. At length he stopped at a lamp post, and reaching out his hands, grasped it. He bowed his head upon his arm, and poured out his heart to the Saviour of sinners, and Christ revealed himself to this poor, miserable man. The burden of sin was gone; and tears of penitence and joy flowed apace.

How long he remained in this position at the lamp post, he does not know. He walked the streets during the remainder of the night, his whole soul filled with joy. As the day dawned, he longed to meet some one to whom he could tell his new experience. He went to various places, but could find no person whom he knew. Early in the morning he went to the Battery, and sat down on the grass. He took a small New Testament from his pocket, and began to read. He was reading the Saviour's own words, and as he read shed tears which he could not restrain. At length a gentleman who had stood silently observing him, said:

"My friend, what little book are you reading?"

"I am reading the New Testament."

"Where did you get it?"

"It was given me at the Fulton street prayer meeting."

"Do you attend the Fulton street prayer meetings?"

"I do. I attend them every day."

"Do they do you any good?"

"Well, I hope they have done me great good. I hope I have found the Saviour."

And then, in his perfectly artless and simple, earnest manner, he narrated the story of the preceding night.

"Well," said the listener, "I have heard much of the Fulton street meetings; I believe they are doing a world of good. Now I will tell you what I want. At ten o'clock tomorrow, I want you to come to my store." And he gave him the name and number in Broad street. They then parted.

Meantime he sought the kind Missionary at the Old Dutch Church. He ran up into the upper Lecture room, where he found him and two or three brethren with him, His whole face was beaming with inward peace. In a few brief words he told the story of the lamp post and the great change.

"Oh! blessed be God" said the Missionary, and in a moment all were on their knees. "Now let us all pray in turn" said he, and he lifted up his voice to God in thanksgiving and praise for his unspeakable mercy to his *dear brother* in Christ, in thus meeting him in his pardoning mercy and renewing grace. One after another followed in prayer, and last the voice of this new creature in Christ Jesus.

Punctual to the minute, the next morning he was at the store in Broad street. There he found a new suit of clothes throughout, which had been provided for him, and a place where he could have constant employment at fair wages.

He is a native of the city of New York—a ship carpenter by trade. He was fourteen years at sea and is forty-six years of age. A few months ago, his case was almost hopeless; he was in the most abject and forlorn condition, and seemed to be sunk past all redemption. Now he gives abundant evidence that he is a new creature in Christ Jesus. "Old things have passed away; all things have become new."

THE DISINHERITED.

The following narrative was given at one of the Globe Hotel meetings by a gentleman from the West. He said that six months ago as he was standing on the west bank of the Mississippi river, a hand bill was put into his hand, inviting him to attend a prayer meeting in the city of New York. " It was the Fulton street prayer meeting. You can scarcely imagine the influence of such a little event as that upon the feelings, course, and eternal well being of an individual. I was invited when one thousand miles away, to attend a Noon day prayer meeting of business men."

He said that on coming to the city, he complied with that invitation, which he had still in his pocket and intended to keep, and he should always have reason to be thankful that he ever attended one of those meetings. He had visited the cities east of us, and he every where found the daily prayer meeting.

He then went on to speak of revivals in places at the West. He spoke of one in particular of great interest. "In a neighbourhood where there was a large population but no church, the people built a large school house, and when it was finished, they resolved to hold in it union meetings for prayer. They were commenced and were largely attended. And when all who came could not get in, they would crowd around the windows to hear. The Lord poured out his Spirit in great power and many were converted.

"Living in the neighbourhood of that school house was a very wealthy and proud infidel. Some of his family were inclined to go to the prayer meeting. He called his family together, and said that if any of them went to that prayer meeting and 'got religion,' as he called it, they were to be disinherited and banished from the house. His wife was included with the children. She had attended, and so had his oldest daughter, which put him in a rage. The daughter continued to go to the prayer meetings and soon found peace in believing in Jesus. When an opportunity was given for those who had a hope in Christ to make it known—she meekly arose and spoke of the 'great change' in her heart and her humble hopes of salvation through a crucified Saviour.

"There were those standing at the window outside who immediately went and told the father of the young lady of the professions she had made. When she went home that night, she met her father, standing in the doorway with a heavy quarto Bible in his arms.

" 'Maria,' said he, 'I have been told that you have publicly professed to night that you have 'got religion.' Is that so?'

" 'Father,' said the girl, 'I love you and I think I love the Saviour too.'

"He opened his Bible to a blank leaf, and pointing with his finger, he said:

" 'Maria, whose name is that?'

" 'It is my name, Sir.'

" 'Did I not tell you that I would disinherit you if you got religion?'

" 'Yes, Sir.'

" 'Well, I must do it. You cannot come into my house.' And, tearing the leaf of the Bible, 'There,' said he, 'do I blot out your name from among my children. You can go.'

"She went to the house of a pious widow lady in the neighbourhood, and heard no more from her father for three weeks. One morning she saw her father's carriage driving

up to the door. She ran out and said to the driver, 'What is
the matter, James?'

" 'Your father is very sick, and thinks he is going to die;
and he is afraid he shall go to hell for his wickedness, and
for the grievous wrong he has done you in disinheriting you
and turning you from his house. He wants you to jump into
the carriage and come home as quick as possible.'

"She found her father sick, indeed, on going home; but
she soon saw he was only sin sick. She talked with him; she
prayed with him; she endeavoured to lead him to Christ. In
three days the father, mother, two brothers and a sister, were
all rejoicing in hope, the whole family together made heirs of
God and joint heirs with Christ to the heavenly inheritance.
How faithful God is to those who put their trust in him."

THE INFIDEL LAWYER.

The meetings at the Globe Hotel were always attended, and
sometimes conducted, by a gentleman whose history is very
remarkable. A member of the New York bar, he was distinguished by his legal acumen and erudition, his eminent abilities, and his infidelity. For many years he has been a skeptic
on every point in religion except the existence of a God. He
was not a scoffer in the common acceptation of the word. He
professed and meant to be a gentleman. But his prevailing
opinion was, that Christians generally did not know enough
to be infidels; that it required a man to have some brains
to be a thorough going, consistent infidel, well able by good
arguments to maintain his position. Such was he.

One Thursday evening in August, he arose and said,
with great modesty of manner: "I am young in Christian
experience. Not many months ago I would have scorned to

have been in this place. Now it is my greatest delight. I looked upon Christ as setting an example of benevolence unexampled in the history of the race. I had no fault to find with his character. He was a *good man*, a man of spotless character, who gave utterance to some of the most beautiful precepts and maxims for human conduct the world has ever seen. So I regarded him *once*.

"But oh! how differently *now*. I did not think of Him as the Crucified, as bearing *my sins* in his own body on the tree, as suffering, the just for the unjust, that he might bring us to God, as wounded for our transgressions, and bruised for our iniquities, and the chastisement of our peace being upon him. I am here a sinner, hoping I have been pardoned through him as my Saviour. The Holy Spirit brought arguments to my heart that made me feel my need of him. And when I was almost in despair, the same Holy Spirit revealed to me his Divine and glorious nature, and his ability to save to the uttermost. Oh! what a sinner I have been, and what a miracle of grace I am. I have no words to express my thankfulness and gratitude, no tongue to tell the preciousness of Christ to me. Ages hence I can tell it better."

This gentleman had long been known to the Missionary of the North Dutch Church, who admired his abilities and his fine social traits, and had often tried to do him good. The first time they personally met was about ten years ago, when Mr. L. found the lawyer at a street corner, far gone in intemperance, bloated, soiled, ragged, unfit to appear in decent society. He ascertained his lodging place and promised to call on him; did so, but could not find him. He repeated the attempt frequently, and at last succeeded on a Lord's day morning in finding him at home, but not yet risen. He left

word he would call after the services. These repeated manifestations of interest on the part of a total stranger awoke a
train of serious thought in the lawyer's mind. He could not
imagine what it all meant, but in his perplexity concluded on
one good thing, viz: that he would not drink anything that
day. In the evening Mr. L. came, invited the lawyer to take
a walk, got him some refreshment, and finally brought him
to a prayer meeting in the Broadway Tabernacle, where the
services affected him deeply, especially the singing, which
revived many old associations.

After service the lawyer held out his hand to his friend,
as he now regarded him, to say "good night," but his friend
insisted on taking him home with him, and at last won his
consent. The poor man having so suddenly broken off from
his cups, suffered a terrible attack of delirium tremens, but
his good friend watched with him through all the unspeakable horrors of the eventful night and the succeeding twelve
hours. At times it seemed impossible for the sufferer to sur-
vive the struggle. But God was gracious to him, and he was
spared. Having passed the crisis, he was restored to himself
and to the community, but not to God. In 1848, he became
a reformed, a sober man, but was far as ever from being a
Christian. Even the beautiful exhibition of Christian love
and self-sacrificing benevolence which he saw in the friend
who sought him out so perseveringly, helped him to break
the chains of intemperance, nursed him through the agony
of deliverance, cheered him with sympathy and put him in
the way of employment, position, and friends, had no effect
upon his fixed, icy infidelity. Nor indeed was that friend at
all instrumental in the change when it did come. Although

he laboured in various ways to this end through the period from 1848 to 1858, yet all without effect.

The means employed were the very last that infidel himself would have imagined. It was the services of a body of Christians, with whose peculiarities he never had had any sympathies, and whom of all others he was most inclined to despise. But this will appear more fully from his own statement, which was written out at Mr. L.'s request and preserved among the archives of the Noon Prayer Meeting.

AWAKENING, CONVICTION, CONVERSION.

"It is past 6 o'clock; clients and office companions have all left for their quiet homes; I only am left alone. In that corner stands my cot, on which I shall presently rest for the night, to renew on the morrow the same dull routine that I have passed today and many days before.

"*Alone!* alone! how shall I occupy or kill the time before it is ten, my usual resting hour?

"I will go out and read the papers; no, I will go over to the saloon, there I shall meet some one with whom to converse about the news of the day, Congress, the State Legislature, Kansas, politics, perhaps the great revival. What interest have I in that? I have examined the subject of religion, the Bible, the Divinity of Christ. I reject the whole. It is not sustained by legitimate testimony. It is all foolishness. Many beautiful sayings are found in the Bible; the benevolence of Christ is above all praise; the writers of the Old Testament had some faint idea of the existence of a spiritual God; it was obscure, imperfect. Once I believed the Bible was a revelation from God, enjoyed religion, did not doubt its reality, was more happy then than now. Those exercised by it now appear to enjoy themselves. I will do nothing to mar their apparent happiness; it will all end in death to be sure, but still I would reverse the sentiment of Paul, 'If in this life only we have hope in Christ, we are of all men the most miserable.' For from observation and experience, I would say, if there be no immortality, no judgment, no heaven, no hell, no eternal *life* for the good; if all religious enjoyments end at death, the Christian's faith, the Christian's hope are greatly to be preferred, as a means of present enjoyment.

"What is that on the desk? Notice of meeting: 'Green street M. E. Church, J.T. Peck, Pastor; religious services every evening this week at half past 7 o'clock; come thou with us and we will do thee good.' Have a good mind to go; have not been in church for a long time; wonder if they will look cross, stiff as they did at 13th street the last time I was there? Will go to church; it will be a good enough place for a couple of hours, then it will be time for retiring. Am in the church close by the door, hope I shall not intrude; will be very civil. They are singing, praying ,singing, preaching. Prayer Meeting announced; shall I go home? 'All are invited to stay;' that does not mean me surely; stay though; leaders in the altar, singing, praying, anxious ones invited to come to the altar. Collections go round; put five cents in the plate; save two shillings for another purpose; felt better on that account went home—slept well.

"It is again past 6 o'clock, P.M.; again alone. What shall I do this evening? There is that Green street Church notice; wonder if M. forgot it; he ought to take it to some place where it may do good. Shall I go again tonight? There is an anonymous letter on the desk. It is dated March 17th, 1838. I read it today for the first time in twenty years. In part is says,

" 'Look to it, that you do not oppose God or stand in his way; look to it lest you may be a stumbling block to sinners, and that the Lord will lead you to reflect and repent, and do your duty, shall be the earnest prayer of a brother in Christ.'

"Good advice: well yes; think I will go to church this evening. If I thought M. had left that notice here for me, I would not go; there is a package of them; he doubtless left them by mistake, or forgetfulness. I will go to meeting; what for? The Bible is no revelation; Christ is no God; God is sovereign, and will do with me just as he pleases in time and eternity. Why should I care? Why fret about that which I cannot help? Hell cannot be much worse than earth. I had nothing to do with bringing myself into this world; if I had been consulted about it, I would not have come. At all events, when I get into hell I shall be rid on one difficulty that torments men here—the fear of death. Have seen animals die; oxen, horses, sheep; seen men die. After death what's the difference between them? They rot and decay alike, alike they are forgotten: what is there about animal man different from animal beast? Nothing, nothing. Is my soul immortal; will it eternally endure? It may be so; what then? It will be a merely spiritual existence, mingling with and lost in the great mass of immaterial existences; no individuality, no consciousness; it will be as it was before my present state. I will go to church again to-night; what will *they* say: I can never be renewed; I shall never again enjoy any religious emotion, how can I? I like to see others enjoy it; there is my best friend L., his whole soul is wrapped up in it; he seems to enjoy it; appears to be happy amidst trials and conflicts enough to drive a man crazy. His circumstances in this life are almost as bad as mine, yet he is always happy, I always miserable. I once did enjoy something of it, the letter reminds me of it; was happier then than now. I was sincere in my devotions then, and believed others were, how did I loose it?

"In church again; occupy the same seat. Went home unsatisfied, restless, sorry, glad, uneasy; thankful that I went to church. Reminiscences of former times crowded upon me: Those happier days, when religion, feeble in it as I was, gave joy to my soul, which many years of subsequent established and sincere infidelity could not wholly obliterate: Those days! I shall enjoy them no more.

"Days passed, weeks passed; the subject was continually upon my mind. I came to that day, that night of agony, of agony unspeakable. Was it a dream? As those days and weeks passed by, daily the meetings in Green street sanctuary were by me attended. Associates joked, ridiculed me for it. M., a new comer into our office, was a religious man; he had left those notices of meetings at Green street purposely for me, (thus I learned). I was glad of it; thought I was not entirely abandoned to infidelity; this thought was strengthened by the members of the Church, who, with kindness, several of them expressed pleasure at seeing me at their meetings. Asked myself often, if there was a possibility for me to become a Christian: no, it cannot be.

"On that day the meeting closed, went home, was alone in my room; old memories revived; distress: anguish: pray I cannot—try—no: it is of no use for me to try; whatever joy there may be in religion for others, there is none for me. The Bible! it speaks not for me. Jesus Christ! he is repudiated, rejected, slain—yes, crucified, but not for me; there was a time it might have been for me; that time is passed: now it cannot be for me; for me? No, no; never: sins of a life-time, how long? How many? All concentrated, real, deep, dark, damning! Oh! memory! my soul sinks under their crushing weight! Sins: sins against myself, man, God, against God; sins terrible in aggregate; more terrible in detail; they enlarge, magnify, all, all in a moment; nothing else but sin; no, nothing. Oh, God! how they cluster around me! The room is dark, darker the gloom upon my soul; in bed, alone, sleep: there is none for me; agony, agony. Is it a dream that comes over me; reality? Yes, reality; Jesus at a distance, Satan near (so it seemed); pray, pray; a voice seemed to say, try—try to pray; no! God appears: still at a distance stands the Saviour; his face fearfully solemn, no signs of anger in it. I think he would, but cannot save me; his countenance alters not. Satan suggests, there is no hope, no hope for me; I feel it—know it; my soul sinks in despair. I look at the Saviour; he seems to smile on me, and say, 'how foolish you are; I have saved others as bad as you. Doubt not my power; when you are in earnest, then look to me.' 'What, me?' 'Yes, you; my office is to save the worst. You have thought and said hard things of me, and now, in all your trouble, you look towards me, but do not trust me; you have not faith in my power to do you good.' Is it possible that I can be saved from this crushing load of sin? Thoughts innumerable, troublesome thoughts, press heavily upon my mind and memory; hours pass—try to be penitent, to believe, to pray; cannot: exhausted—try to dispel these gloomy thoughts! will not go at my bidding. Why am I troubled in this way? It is all nonsense; I cannot be in my right mind, must be crazy: horrible thought! I will go to sleep; shall feel better in the morning; eyes closed; cannot sleep, get up and look out of the window; why, it is daylight; and I have not slept a wink all night. What shall I do? I am not sick; my pulse is quick, but not much quicker than usual. I will go to meeting to-night, yes, to the altar: how absurd! how foolish! Lie down again, mentally saying, 'Blessed Jesus, let me sleep; Satan begone, I am resolved to go!'

"Again awake, two hours have passed. Blessed Jesus I thank thee; canst thou indeed save *me?* Comforting thought, is it *possible?* Jesus have mercy on me; Lord Jesus have mercy on me, even me. Feel strangely, something no language can describe what it is. Jesus is near, Satan stands back; there is hope, faint, faint hope; get behind me Satan: 'whosoever *will* let him come unto me.' I will, blessed Saviour, help me; am helped, I feel it; will believe in Jesus, *my Saviour*; help me to say so Jesus. Father in heaven have mercy on my soul for the sake of Jesus; Spirit of the living God! direct me, help me. Oh help me, even *me.*

"The hour of business has arrived; I am unfit for it, am not happy, hope I shall be: afraid not: in doubt and hope and fear, the day passes to near its close. I will go to the meeting this evening, will not go to the altar, that is not necessary; will confess my sins to God, whilst they are praying; will they pray for me? They would not if they knew my moral position; if they only knew how bad I am, they would not have me in their house. I will give it all up; God knows just how bad I am, he has pardoned some very wicked men. I will go to the altar. Why should I hesitate? Others have there been blessed, why may not I? They will pray for me: if they do God may forgive me: he has pardoned others: the thief upon the cross; denying, swearing Peter.

"Friend L. is experienced in these matters, I will see him and tell him all; he knows me, all my circumstances. He will not believe a word I say, will think it pretence; not a being of my acquaintance but would do the same. None of them will believe that I can repent and be saved. Cannot blame them. I will go and see L.: it will not do any good, he will say I am drunk or crazy; have drank no liquor in months: he will scold me: I will see him, nevertheless; I want his advice.

"God help me—words of prayer, do I mean them? Try mentally to pray; enter L.'s room; none there but he: how do you do? 'Why C. what is the matter with you?' Don't know. 'Are these tears of penitence: It would rejoice my heart to think so.' No answer. 'Come, let us kneel down and pray.' He prayed, prayed for me, 'You pray for yourself.' 'God have mercy,' I heard my voice say. I had mercy; felt it; was relieved; told L. all my feelings and resolutions. 'You have resolved right, you just do it.' Did resolve and was happy; if tears were shed, they were grateful tears.

"As I look back upon that hour of agony and deliverance, with what thrilling emotions can I repeat the words of one of our hymns.

'Tongue can never express
The sweet comfort and peace
Of a soul in its earliest love.'

"From thence, hitherto, I have, by God's grace, rejoiced with thankfulness in the blessed assurance of His willingness and ability to pardon and save to the uttermost all who come to him through Jesus Christ my Saviour."

One of the effects of the publication of this thrilling narrative is seen in the following request, which was dated at Chicago, Sep. 16th, and was signed by the writer's own name.

"The reading of an Infidel Lawyer's Experience has awakened an anxiety for my soul's salvation. Without being an unbeliever, I am still in the bonds of iniquity.

"My object in writing is to solicit the earnest prayers of the members of the Globe Hotel and Fulton street Prayer Meetings, that these bonds may be sundered, and that God in his infinite mercy will convert me and enable me to find peace in believing in Jesus.

"Respectfully,

"—— —— ——"

CHAPTER IV.

Requests for Prayers and for Thanks.

ALMOST FROM THE COMMENCEMENT of the Meeting, it has been customary to receive requests that some particular person or persons should be especially remembered in the supplications of God's people.

In many cases the applicants arise in the midst of the assembly and state the character and circumstances of the object for which they desire intercession to be made. By far the greater portion of the requests come in writing, sometimes anonymously, but often with the name and address of the writer in full. One interesting case of the latter kind is that of a poor outcast who had been brought into a Magdalen Asylum, where she was regarded as one of their "hardest cases." Yet entirely of her own accord, she wrote the note, of which a fac simile (the name for obvious reasons being suppressed), is given on the following page. It need not be said that she was most fervently commended to God—to Him who talked with the impure woman of Samaria, and who allowed one that had been "a sinner" to wash his feet with her tears and wipe them with the hairs of her head.

1858

New York Friday Sept 4th

To the Fulton Street prayer Meeting I desire the prayers of the church I feel that I have been a very wicked girl and that I have led a very bad life and I feel my need of Christ I want to be a Christian

your obedient servant

As the Meeting became more widely known, the requests began to multiply in number and kind. Persons at a distance, hearing of the wonderful answers which had been vouchsafed to the cries of believing suppliants in this assembly, took an early opportunity to secure similar intercessions on behalf of objects which lay near to their hearts, and accordingly sent in their requests in more or less detail. Many of these found their way to the religious press, and thus the practice was bruited abroad over a still wider region, and still greater numbers sought to avail themselves of the prayers of the Fulton street Meeting. And now for months the mail has every day brought these requests, sometimes amounting to as many as thirty in a single day. They come from all parts of the Union, and also from beyond the sea, from towns in England, Germany and Switzerland.

The number of these requests not unfrequently excited deep solicitude in the minds of thoughtful Christians, lest a kind of superstitious feeling might be encouraged in those who send these communications, and a sense of self-complacency be engendered in those who received them. On one occasion, an excellent brother called attention to the subject, and said,

"We are in danger of spiritual pride, because so many eyes are turned to the Fulton street Prayer Meeting, and because so many requests for prayer come to us from all parts of the land. I know that many feel troubled because they come; some, because they occupy too much of the attention of this meeting; others, because they fear that the impression will be created that this is *the* Prayer Meeting above all others, where God hears and answers prayer. Now both these evils are to be guarded against.

"I have been this morning to that upper room where all these requests are kept. I have looked at their contents and character, and I can truly say that my heart was filled with the deepest emotion as I read them. There are requests for prayer there, written as none of us would write them, for none of us could feel as the writers felt when they wrote them. They bear the most unmistakable marks of the anguish and agony of desire for unconverted friends, which only converted persons would feel. There all the relations of life are represented; asking us to pray for brothers, sisters, husbands, wives, fathers, mothers, sons, daughters, acquaintances, friends, churches, parishes, prayer meetings, ministers. Now some of these requests are very touching, as the following from a daughter for an unconverted father. I hope we shall never be unwilling that such requests shall come here, and never feel lifted up because they come.

"This is no Mecca, nor Medina, no Mosque, nor Holy Sepulchre. We feel humbled because they come, not exalted. We lie low before God, while He alone is exalted. Let us cherish the true sprit of fervent humble prayer, and let our faith and prayer go out after all these cases, and bear them up to the throne of the heavenly grace.

"Who can tell the results of our petitions? Who can number or contemplate the value of the blessings which may come upon dying souls in answer to prayer? We have to do with the perishing. We pray for their salvation. We learn here the power of prayer in the signal answers which are given. Everything leads us to prayer."

We proceed to give some specimens of the different classes of these communications:

For Backsliders.
"_____, Georgia, Sept. 5th, 1858.
"The prayers of the Christians of the Fulton street meeting are earnestly implored by a young lady who has been once a backslider from God, and who, in the midst of peculiarly harassing temptations, is now endeavoring to return *fully* to her former rest. Do not—*do not* forget her. 'Lord I believe, help Thou my unbelief.' "

"Central New York, Sept. 13.

"Dear Brother in Christ,

"If it would not be asking too much of a stranger, I would re-quest of the brethren of the Fulton street Church their prayers for my husband, who was once a professor of religion but has wandered far away from duty and God. Also for my only son, who is all that a son need be, but a Christian.

"A Wife and a Mother."

FROM A LITTLE BOY.

"Burk Co., Ga., Oct. 4th, 1858.

"I am a little boy 12 years of age, and tell the truth, and I want to be prayed for.

"Very respectfully,

"___ ___ ___"

FROM A LITTLE GIRL.

"Savannah, Ga., August 28, 1858.

"Dear Sir:

"I am a little girl, and scarcely know how to write to a perfect stranger on so important a subject. But oh! I want to be a Christian so much; …I saw a notice in a New York paper the other day, that God's people would pray for any one who sent on their requests to you at the Fulton street Prayer Meeting; so I thought that I would write, and ask their prayers in my behalf. Perhaps God, in his great mercy, may see fit to answer your prayers, and make an angel of [me].

"___"

FOR A VILLAGE IN ILLINOIS.

"To the Christians of the Fulton street Union Prayer Meeting. Brethren beloved—Our hearts bless and praise God for what he is doing in the churches. *But we are burdened.* We have been engaged in a union prayer meeting for about six months. At first it was well attended, but has since been abandoned by many who profess to love the Lord Jesus. A few of us cannot give it up—the hour of prayer. We are hoping that God will yet hear and answer in a glorious revival, a work which shall bring salvation to the perishing. Because we believe in the efficacy of prayer we address you. Will the dear brethren help us at the throne of grace? Pray for us! that the Holy Spirit may be poured out. In behalf of our community I write."

FOR A CHURCH IN TEXAS.

"Dear Sir: In the name, and for the honour and glory of our blessed Jesus of Nazareth, we humbly and earnestly beseech an interest in those prayers which have been so signally blessed heretofore for others, in behalf of both preacher and people of our little Church of Texana. We long to see the stately steppings of Immanuel in our midst.

"Y'rs in the love of a crucified Redeemer.

"—— —— ——"

FOR A FATHER.

"New York, Sept. 7th, 1858.

"Dear Sir:

"Will you, for our common Master's sake, present the following request at the next prayer meeting. A daughter desired the earnest prayers of God's people for a father, aged, absent, and far from God, that he may, though at the eleventh hour, be brought into the fold of the blessed Redeemer.

"Very respectfully,

"A.S.B."

FOR CHILDREN AND GRAND-CHILDREN.

Once a gentleman presented a request for a lady far advanced in years, and remarkable for her piety; in fact, living close by the gate of heaven. He said, "I have known her for twenty years. She came to the city poor, with herself and her little children to support. She sent them to the Sabbath school. She always kept her children neat and looking respectable. Again and again she has had to wash their clothes on Saturday night, after her children had gone to bed, dry and iron them, so that the children should be enabled to come to Sabbath school the next day. These children always had their lessons. They have had the very best moral training, but they are not Christians. Some of these are married and have children. The sons are in Minnesota. The daughters are here. Now, on behalf of this lady, I ask you to pray for the conversion of her children and grand-children."

FROM A NEW JERSEY PASTOR.

"Men of Business, Men of Prayer, Beloved in the Lord: This is to request you to pray for the conversion of my three sons, now living and doing extensive business in a rising town in Kansas. They give their means with a liberal hand, to advance the worship of God. But oh! they still withhold their hearts. Do, dear brethren, help an aged father to pray for their saving conversion. 'Men of Israel, help!' "

For a Brother.

This moving appeal, of which a fac simile is given on the opposite page, was enclosed to the author some weeks ago. He took the first opportunity to lay it before the Meeting, and the "Sister" may be assured that she did not "carry her burden alone" that day.

For Another Brother.

"A young man now in this room, who is preparing himself for the ministry, asks the prayers of this people in behalf of an unconverted brother who resides in Iowa. That his aged mother, who has reared eleven children, all of whom that have arrived to years of discretion, are now rejoicing in Christ, may be permitted to see her prodigal son return to God before she goes to her final rest."

A Cordon of Prayer.

As a pertinent conclusion to the Chapter, we may cite the cheering remarks made by a brother one day in reference to the number of requests from a distance, and the variety of the sources from which they came. He said that he drew a very encouraging inference from the fact that all parts of the land asked an interest in the prayers here. We might feel sure that all those who asked us to pray for them, prayed for themselves and for us also. And thus it seemed to him as if a cordon prayer were thrown around this meeting.

"The voices of these friends are never heard in this room. But there is a power here which we can scarcely appreciate. It is a power which helps us to prevail in prayer and calls down countless blessings upon us. *Others* pray that *our* prayers may be answered. What a day in which to work!

My dear Friends,

May I ask your prayers for my younger Brother— For years every prayer of my own has been a cry to God for his conversion—but, besides myself, I do not know of one connected with him who cares for his soul." Since reading of your blessed Meetings I have felt that I need bear this burden alone no longer—

I plead for him—plead earn estly for him—not once—nor twice but day after day—Do not forget a soul that has but one in the whole world to pray for it And may God—for Jesus' sake—listen to your supplications, and those of

his Sister—

What encouragement to effort! All over our land the voice of prayer goes up to the heavenly hills from these hearts which know best how to pray. Let us be thankful for the ten thousand times ten thousand silent voices that assist us in our prayers and call down blessings on our heads. I think that herein lies one of the secrets of our success at the throne of grace, and here is a reason for such signal answers to prayer."

It may be well to add, in regard to this subject, that the sending of requests from abroad has never been invited, much less urged by the Committee of the Consistory or the Missionary. At the same time, when such requests are voluntarily forwarded, they are never refused or slighted, but carefully preserved and in due time read from the leader's desk. While the Committee did not originate the custom of sending them from all parts of the country, they are unwilling to put a compulsory end to it.

Requests for Thanks.

The stream of requests constantly flowing in to the Fulton street Meeting is sometimes most agreeably varied by new communications from old contributors. They who before came to ask Christians to pray with them, now ask their brethren to unite in joyful thanksgiving to God for mercies received, like the woman in the parable, who "calleth together her friends and her neighbours, saying, Rejoice with me, for I have found the piece which I had lost." There have been some very pleasing expressions of gratitude and praise sent in by persons who had been at a former period remembered in prayer.

A WIDOW FOR HER SON.

Last winter a widow asked the prayers of the Meeting for a son who had cursed her, and the writer well remembers the thrill which went through those who heard of this unnatural wickedness. Shortly afterwards, she sent a note saying,

"The widow who asked prayers of the people of God for a son who had cursed her, desires to return thanks to a prayer hearing God. Her son has asked *her* pardon. She now requests prayer to be made the he may cry out for pardon from *God.*"

OF A RECLAIMED BACKSLIDER.

"A wanderer from the fold of Christ, who publicly requested the prayers of the Fulton street Noon-day Prayer Meeting, desires to render thanks to God for his blessing in answer to the prayers of God's people: and would request the prayer of this meeting for a son, a seafaring man, who is without hope and without God in the world, and that in his infinite mercy he would bring him to a knowledge of the truth, as it is in Jesus."

FOR A SON'S CONVERSION.

"A widowed father, who some time since asked an interest in your prayers for the conversion of an only son and child, desires now to give devout thanks to God for the salvation of that son; and that it can now be said of him, 'Behold he prayeth.' 'Bless the Lord, O my soul.' "

FOR THE CONVERSION OF THREE MEMBERS OF A FAMILY.

"The thanksgivings and praises of this congregation are requested, in view of what God has bestowed upon a family for whom you prayed. Three of the number have been hopefully converted, and one taken home to glory, leaving a triumphant testimony to the power of God's converting and sustaining grace. Christian friends, there are still three of this family out of Christ, and for whom the departed earnestly prayed that they might be an unbroken family in Heaven. These three are now exercised, and we trust the Holy Spirit is doing His work in the midst of their sorrows. Your united, earnest prayers are still requested for them. God has answered and will continue to answer united prayers. The promise cannot fail. Where two or three are agreed, &c., &c."

FOR THREE SISTERS.

A gentleman, a teller in a city bank, had three sisters for whose eternal welfare he was deeply concerned. Meeting a friend one day, he sent by him a request to the Noon Meeting, asking that prayer should be offered for their immediate conversion. Not long afterwards this friend reminded the Meeting of the circumstance, adding, "and now I am here to say that those three sisters are happy in the pardoning love of Jesus, and are rejoicing with that joy which is unspeakable and full of glory."

FOR A CONVERSION IN THE PENITENTIARY.

One Monday morning a speaker made a statement to this effect: "Three weeks ago I requested you to pray for a young woman in the Penitentiary, whom I had found in my Sabbath visitations to be in a very anxious state of mind. On going down to the Island yesterday, and into the Penitentiary, I found this young woman rejoicing in Christ. She felt that her sins had been forgiven her, and she appears very happy; and

I come into your meeting today to tell you the good news for your encouragement."

FOR A FATHER AND THREE SISTERS.

"Christian Friends—A young man, who frequently attends this Meeting, desired you to return thanks for the conversion of his father and three sisters. All have been subjects of prayer."

THE THREEFOLD MENTION.

In the early part of the year, the prayers of the Meeting were requested for a young man of fine promise, the only child of parents who counted him their greatest earthly treasure. Bright, earnest and active, he was a great favourite with his friends, but being possessed of abundant means and connected with fashionable society, he was leading a life of splendid gaiety and worldliness. Under these circumstances, at the wish of his aged father, his case was mentioned for the first time.

Not long afterwards, a friend, on behalf of the father, called on the Meeting to returns thanks to Almighty God for the conversion of this, his only son. It appeared that the young man had been induced to attend the Noon gathering. There his hard heart was softened. There he experienced the gentle but powerful influences of the Holy Spirit, and there he at last found joy and peace in believing. And now turning his back upon the gay world and its deceitful vanities, he was full of love to Christ and anxious only to do good. Overjoyed in the contemplation of this change, the father felt that he could not go away from New York to his distant home, without offering thanks to the Lord for his unspeakable goodness. And so the case was mentioned a second time.

Some weeks had elapsed when the same friend who had announced the young man's conversion, rose to announce that he slept, yes slept the sleep that knows no waking. By the accidental discharge of a gun, in North Carolina, whither he had gone on business, he was called away without a moment's warning. But his was not the terrible end it would have been, had he died without an interest in Christ. His Christian experience, though short, was enough to prepare him for the heavenly sanctuary and for the society of the blessed. Before leaving New York for the South, he had connected himself with God's people, doing it then for the express reason, as he himself stated, that inasmuch as he was about to reside for a time in a part of the country which was destitute of religious privileges, he supposed, that as a member of the Church he could be more useful in establishing prayer meetings and Sunday schools. Thus his case came before the Meeting a third time.

Surely the thanks of the father would have been even more heartfelt and glowing, had he known that when his son was converted, it was literally Now or Never.

CHAPTER V.

Answers to Prayer.

It was to be expected that when earnest and repeated prayers were so perseveringly offered for specific objects, all this exercise of faith and zeal should not prove vain. Many of the habitual attendants of the Meetings were men given to devotion, abundant in prayers. They prayed in faith. They believed the promises. They expected their fulfillment. They took the fact that God had put it into the hearts of so many of his people to come together day after day to unite in supplication for their common wants, as evidence that there were blessings in store for the believing. This produced unusual fervour and directness in the devotional exercises. Men pleaded, importuned, wrestled, and, as we shall see, prevailed.

This prevalence reacted on the minds and hearts of the petitioners and gave new energy to their subsequent supplications. He who heard them once might well be expected to hear them again. He who was able before to work miracles of grace was still as able for they held with the Apostle that his ability was "exceeding abundantly above all that we ask or think." Some remarkable illustrations of the Faithfulness of God and the Power of Prayer are subjoined.

A FATHER FOR HIS SONS.

"A father," said one of the speakers, "had three sons in distant and different parts of the country, all unconverted. He brought them to the Meeting as subjects of prayer. They were prayed for as only those who believe can pray. What has been the consequence? Three letters have been received from these three sons, who have not communicated with each other—each giving an account of his own conversion."

In a similar case, the father brought before the Meeting the welfare of his son far away in the distant Pacific; and in accordance with his request, fervent prayers were offered. In due season the son returned home, and it was found that he had been converted not only in mid-ocean, but also about the very time that he was made a subject of prayer.

In stating this fact, the father said, "I determined at the time to note down the date of the prayer meeting at which my son was remembered, and I have no reason to doubt that the prayers of God's people were answered. It is wonderful. Away at that distance, God called his attention to religion, convinced him of his guilt, led him to Christ, and the very first thing he had to tell me on landing was, what the Lord had done for his soul. He knew nothing of our prayer meetings. He did not know that he had been made the subject of special prayer, and yet the Lord has made him the subject of special grace."

A Wife for Her Husband.

On the 7th of July last, a lady tarried after the Prayer Meeting to say that she wished to have a request written, to be presented next day for prayer for the conversion of her husband, in Wisconsin. She said she did not know that she would be present, but she would try to be.

She was present, and heard the prayer offered. She then went to stay two weeks at Yonkers. After the lapse of that time, she returned home to Wisconsin. On arriving home, her husband, among other things, said to her, "I have set up family worship since you went away."

"Ah! when did you commence?"

"Some time back."

"Well, I had your case made a subject of prayer at the Union Prayer Meeting, Fulton street, when I was in New York."

"Oh, did you, and on what day was it?"

At first she could not remember the exact day. But after some reflection recalled it, and said,

"It was on the 8th of July."

"Why, that was the very day on which God had mercy on my soul!"

This lady has lately written a letter to a friend here, full of grateful acknowledgments, through whom these facts have been communicated to the Meeting. "Before they call I will answer, and while they are yet speaking I will hear."

"Ask and ye shall receive, seek and ye shall find, knock and it shall be opened unto you."

A Woman's Faith.

This woman, according to the statement by a gentleman one day occupying the leader's chair, was a member of one of the Presbyterian Churches in this city, and as such held in high esteem for her consistent walk and pious zeal. One of the illustrations of her triumphant faith and persevering devotion was contained in the fact, that fully believing in the promises made to earnest prayer, she determined, in an humble earnest way to select twenty of her acquaintances and pray earnestly for their salvation. She kept her resolution, made the selections, prayed without ceasing for their conversion, and in the end had the blessed satisfaction of believing that they had all embraced the Saviour.

The Praying Wives.

A pastor from the interior stated to the Meeting, that in the Church to which he ministered there were twenty-five ladies whose husbands were not pious. They met and spoke one to another of the fact, and of their duty in view of it, and agreed to meet weekly for special prayer for their companions. This practice was kept up, as we understood, for some time. The pastor said that on the Sabbath before he left home for his summer vacation, he had the happiness to receive the last of the twenty-five husbands into the Church.

Another time, a clergyman present spoke of seven praying women, all of whom had unconverted husbands. These wives met statedly for prayer for the conversion of their husbands. They prayed on for ten years, and received no answers to their prayers, and then many were for giving up, discouraged and disheartened from the long delay of the blessing sought. One poor Irish woman, ignorant in the instruction of this world, but abundantly instructed in the teachings of the Holy Spirit, said, "we must not give up our meeting. Do you not know that God is faithful to all his promises? He has never said 'Seek ye my face' in vain." So they prayed on three years more, and all their children were converted, their husbands were converted, the Lord poured out his Spirit in great power, and their friends and neighbours were converted. The Church received large accessions, and the Lord turned almost the whole people to himself.

A SERIES OF ANSWERS.

A young man, who all his life had been averse to either hearing or being spoken to on the subject of religion, was at last impelled to visit the Fulton street Meeting; and through a friend, prayers were offered in his behalf. From that day he experienced an entire change of heart.

Not two days had elapsed ere he sent in a petition that earnest prayer might be offered for an intimate companion, with whom for years he had been associated in sinful pleasures. Prayers were offered; and the next time he met that young friend he found him under deep conviction. Now he is rejoicing in a sure hope in Christ.

Not one week later this same young man offered a request that a fervent appeal might be made to God in behalf of two friends of his, a brother and sister, the only children of a pious widow, whose heart was ever yearning that they might become the children of God. One of our leading ministers arose and offered a special prayer for that brother and sister. The same night both became aware of their need of pardon, and were anxiously enquiring, "what shall we do to be saved?" And now both are come out on the Lord's side.

All these persons had been for years wedded to the fleeting pleasures of the world, and every influence that had been brought to bear upon them to induce them to change their course of life, seemed useless, until these earnest appeals to God were poured fourth.

FORTY-FIVE YEARS OF PRAYER.

An aged mother in Israel, in sending in a request for prayer for a number of grand-children, prefaced it by the following remarkable statement: "Mothers of 'only sons' pray on. For forty-five years, one now present, the mother of an only son, prayed for his conversion, and in this blessed revival the Lord brought him into the visible Church. Pray and never cease."

THE CLERGYMAN'S SON.

At a meeting in October, the following was related as having occurred at a prayer meeting in Philadelphia:

"A written request was handed to the leader of the meeting, that prayer might be offered to the Throne of Grace for the conversion of the son of an aged clergyman. A pastor, well stricken in years, who had long been praying that his own son might be led to see the error of his ways and be brought to the feet of Jesus, rose and made earnest supplication to God that 'this son of an aged clergyman' might be brought to seek redemption through a dying and risen Saviour. His own son, unknown to him, sat in the same room, some distance behind him. This son had been walking through the street, and seeing a great crowd entering the door of the meeting, out of mere idle curiosity was induced to enter and take a seat. And there he heard his own father praying for the conversion of just such a son, and just such a sinner as he himself was. He left the meeting in great distress of mind, could not think of sleep, but walked the streets the whole night. Sometimes he would sit down on the steps of the house whose owner he knew was a Christian, and ponder within himself whether he had not better ring the bell, rouse up the family out of sleep, and beg them to pray for him. It was with difficulty that he could persuade himself that it was an unseasonable hour, and that even though he feared the 'wrath to come,' he must wait till morning before any would pray for him.

"At length morning came. He returned as a prodigal to his father's house, and, through God's grace and mercy, was enabled to humble himself before God, and give up his evil courses, and enlist in the service of Christ, who suffered on the cross, that sinners like him might be saved. That same son of an aged clergyman is now daily employed in persuading sinners, such as he lately was, to come to Christ. That same son, who went into the prayer meeting, attracted out of mere idle curiosity, is now seen daily in the Union Prayer Meeting, ready to take his part in the work and duty of prayer. How changed from the night he walked the streets in agony of mind—now rejoicing with joy unspeakable and full of glory!"

AN OLD MAN'S PRAYER ANSWERED.

The Rev. Dr. Taylor, of Bergen, N.J., at one of the meetings held in the Consistory Room, narrated the following circumstances "as an encouragement for parents to pray for their children:"

"Many years ago an old man, a devoted Christian, started a prayer meeting, which is still continued, having resulted in

many and glorious fruits. As a pastor it was my privilege to
be with him, particularly during his last illness. In several
visits made to this house I found him on the mount, looking
over on to the Land of Promise. Finding nothing seemingly
to mar his comfort or interrupt his joy, one morning as I went
to his dwelling (he was a poor man, and lived in straitened
circumstances,) I determined to satisfy myself whether there
was nothing that gave him any trouble of heart. On entering
his chamber, I asked him in simple terms, 'How are you this
morning?'

" 'Oh, sir,' said he, 'I am well; why should I not be well?
I am near home. Yes, I am near home—near heaven.'

"I took the opportunity to ask him, 'My dear sir, has there
been nothing of late resting upon your heart as an occasion
of trouble?'

"He spoke not a word, but turned his head over to the
wall, and lay so between five and ten minutes; then he rolled
his head back upon his pillow, with his face towards me, and
I saw the tears streaming down his cheeks. 'Oh, yes, sir,' said
he, 'there is one great trouble.'

" 'What is it?' I inquired. 'Speak your whole mind to me
freely.'

" 'Well,' said he, 'I have ten children, and I have prayed to
God for more than thirty years, that I might see one or more
of them converted before I die; but he has denied me. They
are all grown up, as you know, but are not yet Christians.'

" 'How do you get over that trouble?' I asked.

" 'Ah!' he replied, 'I get over it as I get over all other
troubles—by rolling it over upon Christ. I know that God
means to answer my prayers, but he means to wait till I am

gone. But he will do it; I know he will: my children will be converted.'

"This man has been in his grave for fifteen years, and I have watched over his children ever since his death; and now to day I am able to say that seven out of the ten have been born into the Kingdom of God, and that the eighth has also just experienced conversion. This is the answer to his prayer! God did not forget; he only waited; and in like manner he will answer the prayers of all parents who pray in faith for the conversion of their children. Let us, therefore, take courage, and lay hold upon the precious promises of God."

THE WRITER FOR THE SUNDAY PRESS.

One day last summer, a gentleman of considerable gifts and culture, who was connected with one of the Sunday newspapers, wandered into the Meeting and the Consistory building. He can imagine no motive for doing so. He had no love for a place of prayer. He had no interest whatever in religion. He was not conscious even of any curiosity to see or hear what was done in the Noon Meetings. Yet through some unaccountable impulse he came in and took a seat near the desk. In the course of the Meeting he became deeply interested, and when it closed, with tears in his eyes he besought the brethren in charge to tell him what he must do. The Missionary took him to the Rev. Dr. Cutler, the excellent rector of St. Ann's, Brooklyn, who had conducted the Meeting that day. The Doctor, himself deeply moved by the occurrence, opening the Bible which lay before him, read to the stricken sinner the precious invitations and promises of the Gospel, and pointed him to the Lamb of God. The next day the awakened man returned to the Meeting, and sent up to the desk a request for the prayers of God's people. Afterward he expressed the hope that his sins were pardoned by the blood of Christ.

THE CONVERSION OF A SCOFFER.

It has justly been remarked that no instance has yet been known of a man attending any of the Noon Meetings and then going away to mock at and ridicule them. There is in general so much that is solemn and impressive in the aspect of such a meeting, such a spiritual atmosphere pervading the room, that only the most hardened can fail to feel or observe it.

During the last summer, a wicked young man from a western city—a scoffer at all religion—came to New York. Before leaving home, he boasted to his wicked and ungodly companions that he intended to attend the Fulton street Prayer Meetings when he got here, and on returning home they would have some jolly times over the exhibition of what he might see and hear. With such views and feelings, he set out upon his journey.

Long, however, before he got here he became serious— then convinced—and when he arrived he was in great distress of mind. He came to the Prayer Meetings, as he had said, but not to gather materials for scoffing; it was only to ask prayer for himself as a poor, miserable, perishing sinner. Here he found peace in believing, and he went home a converted man—to preach to his associates that very Gospel he had despised.

So God makes the wrath of man to praise him, and the remainder he will restrain.

THE INTENDING SUICIDE CONVERTED.

On the 23rd of last September, the day on which the anniversary of the Noon Meeting was held in the North Dutch Church, a man passing along the street had his attention arrested by the crowds streaming from every direction into the venerable edifice. Curiosity led him to follow them, and entering the building what he saw and heard there changed the whole current of his thoughts. He had been contemplating two awful crimes. But now he was awakened to a sense of his condition. He became convinced of the wickedness of his heart and life. The next day he came to the Noon Meeting and also on the following day, Saturday, when of his own accord and in his own handwriting he sent up to the desk this request:

"The prayers of this Meeting are respectfully requested for G.B——, who has lived all this life in wickedness, and only a few days ago contemplated suicide, and the great crime of murder, in hopes of ending his misery."

The next evening he attended the Prayer meeting, which, conducted in much the same free and spontaneous manner as the Noon Daily Meeting, is held in the lecture room. In the course of the exercises, one of the brethren was delivering a fervent exhortation and urging the duty of repentance, when suddenly he was startled by a despairing cry from one of the audience, "Oh! what shall I do to be saved!" It was the poor would-be murderer and suicide, fallen on his knees and crying for mercy. Just then another poor creature near him rose, and with tears streaming down his cheeks, asked the Meeting to sing for him the well known hymn of Toplady: "Rock of ages, cleft for me, Let me hide myself in thee."

At the conclusion of the exercises, both these men were privately conversed with and directed to go just as they were, with all their load of guilt upon them, to the Lord Jesus Christ. There is reason to believe that both have done so.

G.B., although a very ungodly man, was not a convict or a criminal. But in intention and purpose he was guilty of the highest crimes. He was asked once, "Did you really intend to commit murder and then suicide?"

"I really did."

"Whom did you intend to murder?"

"A woman who has greatly wronged me; and to be revenged I intended to kill her."

"And what then?"

"Suicide and eternal damnation."

"Have you any such feelings now?"

"Not the least."

"What saved you from the crimes you intended to commit?"

"The recollection of my poor mother's prayers." And now his chin quivered, and his eyes filled with tears.

"Have you ever committed a crime, and been imprisoned?"

"Never," said he, with great emphasis and firmness. The author has recently conversed with this man, and found him in a very humble, peaceful state of mind, as far removed as possible from the gloomy, bitter, revengeful, despairing frame in which he was when the anniversary meeting arrested his downward course. He always speaks with great tenderness and gratitude of the prayers and counsels of his mother, who died when he was very young. For a long time the influence of her early inculcations had passed from his mind, so that he was wholly without God in the world, but at the critical moment the memory of them revived and he was made sharer of like precious faith with her own.

CONVERSIONS IN KALAMAZOO, MICH.

The following account was given in one of the Noon Meetings by a gentleman who had been actively engaged in the good work:

"We heard of the wonderful work of grace in this city and in other parts of the land. We thought we ought to share in it and not stand idly by. Still we had no such feeling as was here. We appointed a daily prayer meeting however. Episcopalians, Baptists, Methodists, Presbyterians, and Congregationalists, all united. We appointed our first Union Prayer Meeting in much fear and trembling. We did not know how it would work. We did not know that any body would come. We did not know how the measure would be regarded. At our very first meeting some one put in such a request as this:

" 'A praying wife requests the prayers of this meeting for her unconverted husband, that he may be converted and made an humble disciple of the Lord Jesus.' All at once a stout burly man arose and said, 'I am that man, I have a pious praying wife, and this request must be for me. I want you to pray for me.' As soon as he sat down, in the midst of sobs and tears, another man arose and said, 'I am that man, I have a praying wife. She prays for me. And now she asked you to pray for me. I am sure I am that man, and I want you to pray for me.'

"Three, four or five more arose and said, 'we want you to pray for us too.' The power of God was upon the little assembly. The Lord appeared for us, and that right early. We had hardly begun and he was in the midst of us in great and wonderful grace. Thus the revival began. We number from four hundred to five hundred conversions."

The Prayer Meeting at "Hell Corner."

Few chapters in the history of the Holy Spirit's workings are more surprising than the one under this title, which a gentlemen from New Hampshire related some weeks since in Fulton street. He said: "In the locality of which I speak there are about twenty families, isolated and cut off from all association with the surrounding neighbourhoods. They have no communication with any body beyond themselves.

"These families are distinguished for their profanity, wickedness, gambling, and almost every vice. They have no respect for religious institutions. They are shut out from all means of grace. They are a reckless, hardened set of people.

"On a late occasion, one of these men was in at a neighbour's house, and while there indulged in the most horrid oaths. The woman of the house said to him,

" 'If you don't stop swearing so, I am afraid the house will fall down over our heads.'

" 'Well, I should think,' said the man, 'that you are getting very pious, from what you say.'

" ' Well, I should think it time for some of us to be getting religious.'

" 'If you feel that way, suppose that we have a prayer meeting in your house,' said the man.

" 'Yes, we will have a prayer meeting; we will have a prayer meeting,' chimed in from many voices. And a prayer meeting was agreed upon, and the time was fixed. They got a man to lead the meeting—the only man living in the neighbourhood who had ever been a professor of religion. He was a notorious backslider, and of course answered their purposes all the better for that; for all this was meant as a burlesque upon prayer meetings.

"The time came for the meeting, and all assembled. The backslider undertook to lead the meeting, but broke down in his prayer, and could not go on. They undertook to sing, and could not make out any thing at that. They determined not to give up so. They appointed another prayer meeting, on the next Sabbath at five o'clock P.M. They sent to a deacon of a Church living three miles off, saying, 'that there was to be a prayer meeting at 'Hell Corner,' the common name by which the place was known, on next Sabbath afternoon, and wanted him to come down and conduct it.' The good deacon did not dare to go. He thought it was either a hoax or a plan to mob him. He however spoke to a neighbour about it, and asked:

" 'Had I better go?'

" 'Go, by all means, and I will go with you,' said the neighbor.

" So on the next Sabbath afternoon they went to the prayer meeting at 'Hell Corner.' All were assembled, preparing to give solemn and serious attention to the services.

" 'I had been there but a few minutes,' said the deacon, 'before I felt that the Spirit of the Lord was there.' Four or five of these hardened, wretched men, were struck under conviction at this first meeting. Another meeting was held, and more were awakened. The prayer meetings are continued," said the speaker, "and many of those who were brought under conviction have since been converted, and have become praying men and women. The work is going on with amazing power. At the last meeting heard from, more than one hundred were present. Here was a case where God's Spirit went before any man's efforts—showing us this one fact, that He can work without them. It also shows us the wide-spread range of the Holy Spirit's influences."

PRAYER MEETING AT SEA.
A short time after the burning of the steam ship Austria, a very touching scene occurred in the lower room of the Consistory building.

The 91st Psalm had been read by the conductor of the Meeting, and several prayers offered and remarks made, when a gentleman arose in the congregation and made some very affecting remarks on the subject of faith and trust in God under all circumstances, and by way of illustration made mention of a case on board the "Austria."

He said that he had been informed by some one, for he had no personal knowledge of the parties, that a man whose wife and son were on board that unfortunate ship, had recently been making most diligent enquiry of the rescued passengers who had arrived in our city, trying to learn, if possible, something as to the fate of his wife and son. That on describing his wife to one of the passengers that he had sought out, that passenger thought from the husband's description that he had seen such a woman on board. The husband produced a daguerreotype of his wife, and the passenger immediately exclaimed, "That is the very woman, and God bless you, my dear sir, for it was she that organized a prayer meeting on board, in which my soul was blessed in my conversion."

He then informed the afflicted husband that the last he saw of his wife and son, they were standing as far aft as they could get away from the flames, and when at last the devouring element rushed on them with such force as to be no longer endurable, he saw the wife and mother, with a calm serene countenance, embrace the son, and then both committed themselves to a watery grave.

When the meeting closed, a most affecting coincidence was observed.

A man who sat in the same seat with the one who addressed the Meeting, indeed the very next man to him, clasped his hands, and stood for a moment unable to utter a word, such was his emotion, but at last said, "That woman was my wife, and I, a stranger to every one here, have come in to seek consolation, and to ask an interest in your supplications, that God would assuage my grief, and bind up my broken heart!"

The scene was deeply affecting, and never to be forgotten by those who witnessed it.

Of the rescued passenger referred to, it was said in the meeting, that when in the water, swimming, a pious friend inquired of him how he felt in view of death? He replied, "Perfectly happy; I can now rely on Jesus, and I am safe." And looking up on the ship, he added, "There stands the noble woman, with her son's hand in her's, to whom I owe all my hopes of salvation, for she it was that got up the prayer meetings."

What a consolation to the bereaved husband, to know that the last hours of his devoted, Christian wife, were spent in such acts of love to souls!

The character of the ship's company among whom this zealous lady organized the Prayer Meeting, which was of such blessed influence to at least one soul, may be judged from the following extract from a statement made by Mr. Berry, a member of the Theological Seminary at New Brunswick, N.J., who was one of the rescued passengers:

"On board the Austria there were but few Christians, probably not more than twenty-five. There were some bold, wretched infidels. I saw the boldest and most heaven-defying of them all perish. The day before the disaster, tracts were distributed among the passengers, and were kindly received by most of them; but this man's depravity was not satisfied to receive one and destroy it before our faces, but he stealthily gathered as many as he could from the passengers, and feasted on his shame that he had destroyed them. He was as bold as a lion when there was no danger near; but when God spoke the following day, he trembled at the alarm, and was scarcely able to move.

"I saw him go overboard. He threw out his arms as he lay upon his back on the waves, his eyes seemed as if they would start from their sockets, the writhings of agony were seen in his features; and as he was sinking, the last I saw of him was, he clenched his hands, wringing them in agony, and he just leaving earth for——, oh! for what?"

THE DANGER OF DELAY.

This was once strikingly set forth by a sailor, a Scotchman by birth, who said:

"Will you take a sailor's advice, a stranger sailor, you who are now deciding that at some future time you will be a Christian; will you take a sailor's advice and not delay your choice another hour, but come now and be on the Lord's side. You cannot possibly magnify the danger of delay. You cannot believe it to be half as great as it is.

"I remember when in Panama, one of my brother sailors

was taken very sick. I had previously, on many occasions, urged him to take Jesus as his guide, counselor and friend. But his answer had ever been, 'Time enough yet.' That fearful putting off; that delivering himself up to the power of Satan, who was constantly whispering in his ear, 'Time enough yet,' reached its fearful crisis at last. As he lay sick upon his mattress, his writhings and contortions denoted the fever and pain that were within. But the fever of his soul was causing much more anguish than all his bodily ailments.

"I said to him, 'you need a Saviour now.' 'Oh,' he said, 'I have put off seeking Jesus too long.' I earnestly begged him to look at the cross of Christ and there learn what Jesus had done and suffered, that a poor sinner like him might not perish, but have everlasting life. But he replied, with choking sobs, 'Too late,—too late. Oh!' he cried, 'no rest for me. I am going to some place I know not where. Oh! I know not where!' His head fell back upon the pillow. I cried, 'Ned, are you dying?' But all I heard was through the gurgling in his throat—'no rest'—and my dying shipmate was gone."

Another touching incident he related as intimately connected with his own conversion, bearing upon the danger of delay. It was at his own home. He had a very pious God-fearing mother, who had never neglected any opportunity which offered, to impress upon his young mind the urgent need of seeking a Saviour in his youthful days, but he had constantly neglected to pay more than a passing attention to his mother's admonitions, until one Sabbath morning his mother invited a young girl, a neighbour's daughter, to accompany them to the house of prayer. She replied in a light and trifling manner, "Oh! no, I cannot go until next

Sunday. I shall have a new bonnet them; my old one is too shabby." "Alas! that next Sabbath never came for her. On Monday she was taken quite sick. On Wednesday she died. My mother told me, with streaming eyes, as she came home from watching at her bedside, 'Emma is gone; and gone, I fear, without conversion.' This was so sudden, so unexpected, that it woke within my heart the cry, 'What must I do to be saved?' And blessed be God, that cry was not made in vain. Jesus had mercy on my Salvation. Oh! come to him, all you who need the soul. He has been to me ever since that time the Rock of saving grace of a dying risen Saviour! Will you take a sailor's counsel? Will you come? God is calling you. Come now."

LITTLE CHILDREN SAYING GRACE.

"It had been noticed," said a speaker, "that something was the matter with four little children from the same family, in one of our public schools. One of the teachers inquired what the matter was, and she ascertained that these lovely little children were suffering from lack of food; that all they had to eat for days was a crust of bread and water. They had come to school with no better. They were German children, and their parents were unable to obtain food for them.

"This teacher, who had ascertained the facts, went to the head teacher and communicated them to him. He sent home immediately, and had a good dinner prepared for them. He then took them to his own house. On arriving there the youngest refused to go in. He said he did not know what kind of a house it was, and he did not like to go into a house without his mother knowing and approving of it. Finally, after very much persuasion, they got them all into the house. They took them to the parlour; there was an abundant meal set out. They seated them at the table; they urged them to eat: they could not persuade them to touch a mouthful. Finally it was resolved to leave these little children alone; perhaps they would eat then. The lady of the house paused at the door, and looking through the crack, what was her surprise to see the oldest little boy put his two little hands together, and say grace—asking for God's blessing, and thanking him for his mercies. May we not all learn a lesson," said the speaker, "from these little children, who, though they were starving, refused to eat till they had first acknowledged God's hand in the food provided."

"IN A HURRY TO BE A CHRISTIAN."
Careless readers of the narratives which have been given, may conclude that the missionary work in the Consistory building is always prosperous; that conviction is always followed by conversion. Alas! it is not so there any more than elsewhere. The following report of a case was published a number of weeks since. It respects a man who was deeply agitated respecting his soul, and thought that he had good reason to be.

"He had been a man of such a course of life that he had much to repent of. He had been a great transgressor—profane—idle—dissolute—intemperate—a hater of religion and all its duties and requirements—a disbeliever in much that is called religion. He had lived a hardened, ungodly life, till he chanced to stray into one of the Fulton street Meetings.

"He came up to the upper lecture room in great trepidation of mind. He wanted to find some place where there was a temperance pledge. He wished to sign it. He wanted to begin, at the beginning—and the first thing was to quit the abomination of strong drink. This was the beginning of 'Let the wicked forsake his way,' and then he hoped he should be able to forsake every thing else that was wicked. He appeared to be in great haste. He said he was 'in a hurry to be a Christian.' This surely was according to the Scriptures, and yet he seemed to be wholly taught of the Holy Spirit.

"We saw him a few days after this. He had been faithful in coming to all the meetings. He had been faithful to his pledge of total abstinence. He was very jealous of himself. His great fear was, that some old 'evil companion' would get power over him—would get him to drink just one drop; then all would be gone, soul, body,—all would go to hell together. He said his continual prayer was, 'Lord! hold thou me up and I shall be safe. I cry to God continually, for I feel that God must help me or I shall fall. No man can realize the power of this appetite, who has not felt it. I must be a Christian to be safe.' "

It would be pleasant to be able to relate that one so humble, so enlightened, so conscious of his dependence, had persevered and been saved. But it is not in our power. It is not known that he has found the Saviour. It is known that once at least, after the occurrence of what is recorded in the foregoing extract, he fell into his ruinous sin. There is reason to fear that he illustrated his own declaration, "I must be a Christian in order to be safe." Not having the safeguard of renewing grace, he fell, fell, perhaps, to rise no more.

Yet even here there is no reason to despair. Many men have fallen repeatedly, and yet have been finally raised by God's grace so as to stand even to the end. Indeed, one of the most important lessons taught by the recent displays of

Divine power and mercy, is that no case is to be given up as hopeless. We cannot read the counsels of Him who "giveth not account of any of his matters;" we cannot possibly know when any man's day of grace is past; and therefore to us, "while there is life, there is hope." The prayers and efforts of Christians for any unconverted person should cease only with the cessation of his vital breath.

CHAPTER VI.

The Noon Meeting in Philadelphia.

AMONG THOSE WHO ATTENDED the first business men's prayer meetings in New York was a young man not twenty-one years of age. As good had resulted from these meetings in New York, why might not equal good be done through their instrumentality in Philadelphia? Surely it was worth the effort. Some of his fellow members of the Young Men's Christian Association, with whom he conversed, being of the same opinion and promising their cooperation in the matter, he applied to the trustees of the Methodist Episcopal Union Church, for the use of their lecture room. The request was promptly complied with, and the first Noon Prayer Meeting in the city Philadelphia was held in the Union Church, November 23d, A.D. 1857.

For a time the response on the part of the business men was far from encouraging; thirty-six being the highest number present, and the average attendance not exceeding twelve.

At length it was deemed expedient to remove the Meeting to a more central position, and the ante-room of the spacious Hall of Dr. Jayne having been generously granted by him for this purpose, the first meeting was held there February 3d, 1858. Even there the increase in numbers was very gradual indeed; first twenty, then thirty, forty, fifty, sixty persons. So little in the first instance did the kingdom of God come by observation.

But now almost as in an instant the whole aspect of affairs underwent a most surprising change. Instead of reproducing the scene from memory, permit me to quote the description given at the time by an intelligent and competent witness.

"By Monday, March 8th, the attendance in the smaller apartment of the Hall had reached three hundred, and by the next day it was evident that many were going away for want of room. The persons present, with much fear of the result, yet apparently led by Providence, on Tuesday, March 9th, voted to hold the Meeting the next day at twelve o'clock in the large Hall. It was our privilege to be present at that time, Wednesday noon. The Hall has seats for twenty-five hundred people and *it was filled*. The next day it was filled again, with the galleries, and it was obvious there was not room for the people. The curtain was therefore drawn away from before the stage, and that thrown open to the audience. The next day, Friday, the partition between the smaller and the larger rooms was taken down, and the Hall from street to street thrown open.

"The sight is now grand and solemn. The Hall is immensely high. In the rear, elegantly ornamented boxes extend from the ceiling in a semi-circular form around the stage or platform; and on the stage, and filling the seats, aisles and galleries, *three thousand souls at once on one week-day after another, at its busiest hour, bow before God in prayer for the revival of his work.* The men and women, minister and people, of all denominations or of name, all are welcome—all gather.

"There is no noise, no confusion. A layman conducts the Meeting. Any suitable person may pray or speak to the audience for *five minutes only.* if he does not bring his prayer or remarks to a close in that time, a bell is touched and he gives way. One or two verses of the most spiritual hymns go up, "like the sound of many waters;" requests for prayer for individuals are then made, one layman or minister succeeds another in perfect order and quiet, and after a space which seems a few minutes—so strange, so absorbing, so interesting is the scene—the leader announces that it is one o'clock, and punctual to the moment a minister pronounces the benediction, and the immense audience slowly, quietly and in perfect order, pass from the Hall! Some minister remaining, to converse in a small room off the platform, with any who may desire spiritual instruction.

"No man there, no man perhaps, living or dead, has ever seen any thing like it. On the day of Pentecost, Peter preached; Luther preached: and Livingston, Wesley, and Whitfield! Great spiritual movements have been usually identified with some eloquent voice. But no name, except the Name that is above every name, is identified with this Meeting. 'Yes,' said a clergyman, on the following Sabbath, 'think of the Prayer Meeting this last week at Jayne's Hall, literally and truly unprecedented and unparalleled in the history of any city or any age; wave after wave pouring in from the closet, from the family, from the Church, from the union prayer meetings, until the great tidal or tenth wave rolled its mighty surge upon us, swallowing up for the time being all separate sects, creeds, denominations, in the one great, glorious and only Church of the Holy Ghost.' "

But even these descriptions fall short of the real extent of religious feeling in the city at large. Jayne's Hall, immense as it was, was not the only place where Christians of every name met for the purpose of united prayer. Towards the close of that same Pentecostal week, a Union Prayer Meeting was called in a church conveniently situated in the northern part of the city. At the hour appointed, some twenty persons might be seen slowly making their way through the unbroken snow drifts to keep their faith with God and with each other. But from the very moment that they crossed the threshold it was manifest that God was with them of a truth, and that the blessing was "coming" to them also.

On Friday afternoon it came with all its fullness; the large lecture room, capable of holding some five hundred persons, was full to overflowing. The number of requests for prayer on the table was so great that the leader only looked at them with wonder and did not pretend to read them. "Doubtless," he said, "we all feel just in the same way for our unconverted friends and relatives. For my own part I must ask you to pray for my four sons!" "For my two sons and daughter," said a second. "For my father," said a third. "For my husband," said a lady with a tenderness and energy that thrilled us to our very souls; and thus in less than three minutes perhaps, a hundred similar requests were presented throughout the whole room.

Then as with one accord we lifted up our voices and wept together. The place was indeed a "Bochim," and of all the scenes that have been witnessed throughout this whole revival, perhaps there was none more perfectly characteristic and overwhelming. A few days subsequently, at this same meeting, the people of God as by a common impulse rose to their feet, and there standing before the Lord, solemnly consecrated themselves afresh to his service. The history of that meeting "in souls renewed and sins forgiven," would make a volume of itself.

At the close of one meeting a lady approached a little group of ministers and others, and called one of them aside to speak with her. "I could not find it in my heart," she said, "to leave this room, until I told what God had done for my soul. I came here this afternoon in darkness, heavily burdened with my sin, and well nigh in despair; but during the third prayer I felt as if I could believe in Christ; peace came to my soul, and *now I must go home and tell mother.*" The tone of voice, the expression of countenance, the tears rolling down her cheeks, and joy meanwhile beaming from her eyes, it is utterly impossible for us to describe. Conversion was to her a change and *real*, as for one asleep to awake, for one who was blind to be made to see, for one who was a captive in darkness and a dungeon to be made free.

The lecture room having become too strait for the multitude of worshippers, similar union prayer meetings were established further west and north in the afternoon, and also in the Handel and Hayden Hall at noon, the attendance at the latter place amounting at times to a thousand or twelve hundred persons. Taking all the union prayer meetings together, independent of the regular Church prayer meetings in the evening, the number of those who daily met for prayer about this time was at least FIVE THOUSAND.

In connection with the Union Prayer meeting, as if by common consent, union preaching was also established. That all might feel equally free to attend, the favourite places for such preaching were the great public halls, such as Jayne's, Handel and Hayden, and the American Mechanics', all of which were freely tendered by the proprietors for the use of the people without expense. The time appointed for these services was usually on an afternoon of a week day, or at such an hour on the Sabbath as would not interfere with public worship in the churches. Two sermons in this course, by Rev. Dudley A. Tyng, were very memorable, especially the last, where the congregation numbered more than five thousand persons, and where "the slain of the Lord" were more perhaps as the result of a single sermon than almost any sermon in modern times.

Meanwhile the increase of attendance at public worship on the Sabbath, and the number of churches opened for services during the week, was beyond all precedent. During the latter part of the winter, rarely indeed would you pass the lecture room of an evangelical Church in the evening, that was not lighted up for prayer or preaching. Sometimes even the main body of the church itself was not able to accommodate the multitude of worshippers.

In some these services had commenced months or weeks before and were only continued. In others they were now held for the first time. In nearly all, there were the manifest indications of the presence and power of the Holy Ghost. The action of the Union Meetings upon the Churches, and of the Churches upon the Union Meetings, was reciprocally delightful and profitable. No rivalry, no collision, the revival spirit was one and the same every where; the same spiritual songs, the same fervent intercession for sinners, the same earnest invitation to come to Christ that they might receive the Life Eternal.

While such wonders as these were occurring all through the city, public attention and interest were awakened in no ordinary degree. In vain was an occasional cry raised here and there of "priestcraft," "enthusiasm," "fanaticism." No definition of these terms seemed at all applicable to the case in hand. In vain did the boldest of the transgressors endeavour to rally an organized opposition. The disposition to cease from the instruction that causeth to err, left the synagogues of Satan deserted and desolate.

In vain was every possible expedient resorted to to involve the followers of Christ in angry and unprofitable controversy. Speaking the truth in love, and believing that the best way to refute error was to teach the truth, they humbly relied on the Holy Spirit to make the truth manifest in every man's conscience. The worse the man, the more did they pity him. The greater the enemy, the more did they pray for him. On one occasion, at the Noon Prayer Meeting, Nena Sahib himself was proposed as a subject of prayer, and by whom of all other persons in the world, but by a Christian mother, whose own son was one of the Missionaries so foully murdered by him.

As an evidence of the reality and the extent of the revival, the number of conversions during the year, in Philadelphia, may be safely estimated at ten thousand; one denomination having received three thousand, another eighteen hundred.

Perhaps never, in the entire history of the Church, since the days of the Reformation, were the winds and waves that too often disturb the bosom of the Church, more thoroughly subdued and hushed to rest, than during the few days that intervened from the death of our beloved brother Tyng, until his remains were committed to the tomb. Once more Christianity seemed to reach her true summit level. The kind, fraternal cooperative spirit that had thus been developed must of necessity find some appropriate sphere in which to manifest itself. It looked for a field in which to enter, and lo! it found it at once in that of the "Union Missions." Union in prayer and effort for the conversion of men; charity in allowing them afterwards to join such denomination as would seem most natural to them. The history of the "Union Tabernacle," the "Big Tent" for field preaching, and of the Firemen's Prayer Meeting, wonderful as they are, are only the ripened fruits of the little germ that was Divinely planted in the Fulton street Prayer Meeting, New York. From that hallowed spot it was that the cry first went forth: "The Lord has risen," which since that time has been heard all over the land.

G.D., Jr.

CHAPTER VII.

General Reflections.

I. No devout or thoughtful mind can review the history which has been given, without being irresistibly led to the conclusion, expressed by the words of the Psalmist upon a different occasion: "THIS IS THE LORD'S DOING; IT IS MARVELLOUS IN OUR EYES."

It is easy to trace the hand of Providence in every step of the course we have narrated. The appointment of the Missionary just at the period when it was made, the upspringing in his mind of the conception of a business men's prayer meeting, its peculiar features, the state of the times prompting men to pray, the absence of any unusual attractions, the extraordinary rapidity with which mid-day meetings for prayer were multiplied; all these indicate the immediate agency of the Most High. The Lord alone was exalted in that day. There is no room for human merit to insinuate itself.

A few men, by no means eminent for influence or position, meet for prayer in the third story of a building in the heart of a dense population devoted to material pursuits; and within a hundred days similar meetings are counted by scores and their attendants by thousands. No new revelation is made or pretended; no mighty machinery set in motion; no Whitfield or Spurgeon appears in the pulpit; no startling tales of conversion are reported, for these followed rather than preceded the popular movement. Yet the minds of men as if by one consent, are turned to the place of prayer. No sooner is a room opened for the purpose than it is filled. And such rooms are opened in every part of the city—a circumstance which was blessed of God to one man's soul in this singular way: A resident of Vermont was in town for some secular purpose, and was struck by the number of signs he saw in different parts of the city, bearing the usual inscription, "Business Men's Prayer Meeting, for one hour," etc. In Fulton street, in John street, in the lower part of Broadway, in the upper part of it, in Ninth street, etc., etc., he was met by the same call to prayer. Now he did not attend one—not one of these Meetings, but after his return home he could not get the thought out of his mind, that business men in New York were in such large numbers meeting for prayer at mid-day. That thought finally was the means of his conversion.

But besides the public gatherings of this nature, there were innumerable private ones wherever any number of men or women were habitually assembled on the same premises—a fact, of which the following remarkable illustration was given at the time in the public prints:

"At one of our large restaurants, a gentleman had taken out a book to read while his dinner was preparing. On the arrival of the waiter with the articles he had called for, he laid down his book, when the waiter said, 'Is that a Bible, sir?' 'No,' was the reply. 'Do you want a Bible?' 'Yes, sir, I should like to have one.' The gentleman promised to bring him one the next day. He did so, asking the waiter whether he attended any of the daily prayer meetings. 'No, sir, we have not time, being engaged here from early in the morning until late in the evening; but at ten o'clock we close, and then all the waiters have a prayer meeting in one of the rooms in this house, and we know that good has resulted.' "

Now on what known principle of human nature shall this be accounted for? Some have attributed it to fashion. But who set such a peculiar fashion, and how came it to be so generally followed, when no ordinary inclination of the carnal heart was appealed to? For surely it will not be claimed that worldly men, however upright or amiable, have any natural proclivity for a simple prayer meeting. Others endeavour to explain it by saying that it was an awakening of the religious sensibility in men's hearts. But this is the very thing we are enquiring after. How came that sensibility to be thus suddenly and widely awakened? No one believed the end of the world to be just at hand; no baleful comet excited the fears of the ignorant or the superstitious; no cunning appeals to popular prejudice subjected the multitude to the control of unseen masters. None of these, nor any thing like them, can be pretended for a moment. A third class said, and with much apparent show of reason, that this result naturally followed from the pecuniary pressure of the times, driving men to religion as their only solace. But does adversity always lead men to God? Is it not, alas! common to see both individuals and communities acting after the example of that wicked king of old, of whom the emphatic record runs, "And in the time of his distress did he trespass yet more against the Lord: this is that king, Ahaz." Besides, in the year 1837, there was a commercial revulsion, quite as wide-spread and unexpected as that of 1857, and tenfold more disastrous; yet there was then no unusual turning to religion, no mighty movement of the popular mind, no upheaving of the foundations. The people as a whole were far more intent upon examining into the political or economical causes of the pecuniary pressure, than into its spiritual bearings, or its final cause as ordained in the providence of God.

No, no; that movement which far more than the opening of China, or the re-conquest of India, or the laying of the Atlantic Telegraph Cable, has rendered the present year memorable; which without exaggeration may be emphatically called the event of the century; which has been more like a literal reproduction of the scenes of Pentecost than any other which has taken place since the tongues of fire sat upon the heads of the Apostles; that movement can justly be traced to no human or earthly source. Look at it as we will, in its commencement, its progress or its results, the conclusion is still the same. THIS IS THE FINGER OF GOD. The contact of the Divine author with his work was so direct and close as scarcely to allow the human instrument to appear, much less to become prominent. The only unusual instrumentality was that of which this volume describes the origin—Daily Union Prayer Meetings. Yet prayer is always the confession of want, the resort of weakness, the expression of dependence. As well might the way-side beggar make a merit of stretching forth his hand for casual alms, as Christians attribute inherent worth to their devotions, whether individual or collective.

Prayers are indeed the *causa sine qua non*, but never, never the *causa qua*, of spiritual renovation, and least of all, of a general awakening like that which has just visited so large a part of Christendom.

This is the work of him who rides upon the Heavens by his name JAH. As he looses the bands of Orion and brings forth Mazzaroth in his season; as he, with the breath of spring, dissolves the icy bands of winter, renews the face of the earth and clothes all nature with verdure, freshness and beauty; so He alone breathes upon the cold, torpid, insensible hearts of men, and says: Receive ye the Holy Ghost. Then Lazarus in his tomb feels the pulsations of returning vitality. The dry bones leap up covered with flesh and sinews. The dead in trespasses and sins are quickened into new life. Only He who first created the human spirit can re-create that spirit after its fall and decay, so that the Divine image shall once more be reflected in its various faculties and operations. And if this be true in the case of a single individual, much more is it true when the question is of great masses convulsed as if by a moral earthquake, of whole communities swayed by a single impulse, of nations born in a day!

One of the distinguishing characteristics of this work, is not only that the Lord has done it, but that it is so manifest that he has done it. His people have been called, like Israel at the Red Sea, to stand still and see the salvation of God. Their enemies have been compelled to say, "The Lord his God is with him, and the shout of a king is among them." The extreme frailty of the earthen vessels in which the heavenly treasure was put, showed, as if with the force of demonstration, that the excellency of the power was of God and not of man. Thus has the pride of human glory been signally stained. Thus have Christians been taught to sing with new emphasis the song of the old Psalmist, "Not unto us, O Lord, not unto us, but unto Thy name give glory, for Thy mercy and Thy truth's sake."

II. The true theory of CHRISTIAN UNION has been remarkably developed in the progress of the Noon Prayer Meeting in Fulton street and the innumerable meetings elsewhere, which took the same type.

The Noon assembly as originally planned by Mr. Lanphier and afterwards successfully carried out, was designed for Christians as such, without respect to denominational distinctions. They who came were not expected to deny or to ignore their peculiarities as members of distinct branches of the Church militant, and still less to forsake their customary ecclesiastical associations for the purpose of forming a new one as a sort of eclectic society, retaining the best features and dropping the worst of all the rest. No such chimerical idea was entertained. On the contrary, nothing was said of denominational views. Men were invited to come simply as those who felt their need of prayer and were willing to subtract an hour from secular duties for the purpose.

As such they came with remarkable unanimity and cordiality. Arminians and Calvinists, Baptists and Pedo-Baptists, Episcopalians and Presbyterians, and Congregationalists and Friends, sat side by side on the same benches, sang the same hymns, said Amen to the same prayers, and were refreshed and comforted by the same exhortations. The simple rule, "No CONTROVERTED POINTS DISCUSSED," sufficed to prevent any topic or tone being assumed by one to the annoyance of others; sufficed, I say, with the occasional and rare exceptions, which really are scarcely worthy of notice. The glory of Christ, the progress of his kingdom, the wants of perishing souls, the need of the Holy Spirit, the desirableness of greater conse-cration to the Master—these and kindred themes furnished sufficient occupation to mind and heart. And while dwelling on these, other points faded from view, and the worshippers felt that they were brethren, and as such freely mingled their songs and sympathies and tears and hopes and vows.

The natural consequence of this was a warmer spirit of Christian love and a heartier union in all common and gen-eral efforts for the good of souls. The participants in these services understood each other better than they did before. Prejudices and misconceptions were removed by close and friendly contact, and while each held his own peculiar views of disputed points as strongly as ever, yet they saw and felt that outside of these there was a common ground where all could act in concert and harmony. This impression was made the more deeply because it was undesigned. It was no part of the original object of the Noon Meeting to unite Christians of various names more closely together. Yet this was the result. For when men had experienced the blessed influences of the service, had felt that the Spirit of God was there, had found their highest spiritual joys renewed, and received a fresh unction from above, their hearts were ir-resistibly drawn out toward each other. They became more tender of each other's feeling, interests and good name. They rejoiced in each other's prosperity, and sorrowed in each other's adversity. They could not but feel that although they were distinct regiments, with different uniform and equipments, still they all belonged to one great army, were under the same illustrious Captain, and fought against a common foe, even the zealous and implacable enemy of God and man.

Thus an incidental, but very important part of the usefulness of the Noon Prayer Meetings is seen to lie in the spur and stimulus which they gave to this sacred unity. Christians have felt since as they did not feel before. Not that the bands of denominational organization and attachment have been relaxed. This was neither sought nor desired. But men have learned, while firmly holding their own views, to respect those of their brethren; while cultivating their own field, to look with entire sympathy upon the labours of others; while rejoicing in the particular ecclesiastical name they bear, to feel that there was one yet nobler, which, while it leaves out of view no fundamental truth, yet is able to include every child of Adam who ever learned to lisp the story of the Cross. This is the name CHRISTIAN.

III. The place of the LAY ELEMENT in the diffusion of the Gospel, is another point which the Noon Meetings have contributed to bring out and establish with precision and clearness.

In these services, the responsibility for interest and success has been made to rest directly upon the laity as such. It is true, clergymen were not excluded, but on the contrary, were gladly welcomed. Very many of various names have attended from time to time and have often added largely to the interest and instructiveness of the occasion by their fervent intercessions and their judicious and pointed addresses. Still the hour and the place of meeting show that no reliance was placed upon any special agency and influence of the clergy. The assembly was designed for persons actively engaged in secular pursuits—that they might be refreshed amid the toils and cares of life, by a daily season of prayer and praise, and, in accordance with the Apostolic precept, "Exhort one another daily," by simple unstudied words of mutual exhortation. This end, we have already seen, was fully accomplished. Christians found it good to be there. They loved the place of mid-day prayer. They found their hearts cheered and their souls edified by the exercises. Simple as these exercises were, free from any factitious excitement, destitute of aught which could minister to other than religious tastes, they were found to possess a charm which induced men to make it a point to attend them and to participate actively in them, as the Lord gave ability and the opportunity.

Requests for prayers for impenitent or awakened persons, presented sometimes by the parties themselves, but more generally by their friends, began to multiply. And the voice of intercession became daily more tender and tearful and urgent and importunate. God's people wrestled with Him like the patriarch of old, and at times the place became a Bochim.

Now it was impossible for men with Christian hearts to join sincerely in such supplications, and then sit still. It was impossible for souls touched with the love of Jesus to have the condition of Christless persons brought habitually before them, and yet remain unconcerned and inactive. The fire burned within, their own minds got into a glow, and out of the abundance of the heart the mouth spoke. They began to work for Christ and for the conversion of sinners. They conversed in private with impenitent friends, they invited them to the Noon Meeting, when that overflowed they instituted other meetings of a similar kind, they distributed tracts and handbills and books, they made it part of their business to labour in one or all of these ways, and they expended time and pains and money in such labour.

Of course it is not meant that this was now done for the first time; for earnest Christians have always been engaged more or less in doing good in these or in similar ways. But the thing was now done on a broader scale, by a larger number of persons, and with a greater proportion of immediate success. The Noon Prayer Meeting was a laymen's meeting from the commencement, and its success acted directly upon laymen in revealing to them the immense amount of unemployed talent which lay wrapped up in a napkin, and in stimulating them to an active, diligent and conscientious use of their faculties and opportunities.

The too common notion that the minister, with possibly the elders and deacons, is to do all the work in applying the Gospel to the hearts of men, and that the main body of believers are to be gently wafted to heaven "on flowery beds of ease," was effectually broken up. The true conception of the Church, given so often by the Apostle, as a living organism composed of various parts, each of which has its appropriate function, the performance of which is indispensable to the integrity and perfection of the whole, was beautifully brought out and exemplified.

The Christian is to get good by doing good. He is to be watered himself by watering others. He is to work in the vineyard. He is to follow the example of Him who went about doing good. He is not to go to Heaven alone, but to take others with him. Carrying in his heart from day to day a fresh sense of his obligations to the One who bought him with his blood, he is to labour to bring others to the service and praise of that blessed Master. In the most humble and touching of all the penitential Psalms, no sooner does the royal penitent obtain a ray of hope and feel the hand of Divine forgiveness healing his broken bones, than he announces his purpose to point others to the same great source of deliverance and blessing: "Then will I teach transgressors they ways, and sinners shall be converted unto thee."

Such is always the natural instinct of a renewed nature. "Come and hear, all ye that fear God, and I will declare what he hath done for my soul." Too often this spontaneous impulse is crushed by timidity, the fear of man, a false shame, or a foolish regard to conventional usages. Then, by a natural reaction, faith is weakened, love grows cold and the sense of eternal things declines in vividness and power. And great is the loss to the believer himself and to the Master's cause! But if it be fully seen that it is part of the normal conception of a Christian, that he should have the salvation of others always as a distinct and well defined object before his mind; if believers act habitually under the conviction expressed by James, "He which converteth the sinner from the error of his ways shall save his soul from death, and shall hide a multitude of sins," then there is a vast gain on all sides.

There is gain to the Christian labourer, for, not to mention other considerations, the blessed work is its own reward. And there is gain to the Master's cause, for such labour is never in vain in the Lord. One may sow, and another reap; but in the end, "both he that soweth and he that reapeth shall rejoice together."

IV. Another truth repeated and signally verified in the Noon Meeting, is the POWER OF PRAYER.

As has been related, the Meeting arose out of a fresh

and vivid sense of the present value of daily prayer amid life's cares and toils. The same experience was continued, and enjoyed in a still larger measure by those who used this means of grace. A joyful feeling of relief, refreshment and peace was diffused through their souls, when they thus turned aside from secular pursuits, and held communion with God "in humble, grateful prayer." Care was lightened, burdens were removed, the damaging taint of worldliness wiped away and a sweet sense of the Divine presence shed abroad in the heart. It was experience of this kind which at an early period drew many Christians of various denominations to the Consistory building. They were drawn there by a spiritual attraction, which is always irresistible to a living Christian. Just as the inhabitants of the air and of the sea love the element in which they live and move, so do renewed hearts love the atmosphere of a praying circle. There they are at home. There they breathe freely. There they enjoy life.

But this effect of prayer—its influence at the time upon the offerer—although great and important, is not the only, nor even the principal end which suppliants seek. There are theories of so-called Christianity, which maintain this soulless dogma, holding that it is impossible for human petitions to affect the stately march of the Divine purposes, and that therefore the sole function of prayer is to bring the suppliant's mind into a proper frame by his conversance with God and eternal things. But it may well be questioned whether any human being ever did or could pray under such a conviction. He may have begun with this view, but if he continued, inevitably the heart would get the better of the head, and the man would plead as though he were directly seeking and expecting some gift from above. It is only when the direct benefit of prayer is before the mind, that its indirect advantages are obtained. Reverse the order, and make the latter the primary objects of desire, and they are lost. The soul cannot be worked up to genuine feeling through an idle form, the very terms of which must all the while appear a solemn mockery.

The attendants at the Noon Meeting were not philosophers or theorizers, but humble believers. They put implicit faith in the Divine word. God having been pleased to appoint a fixed connection between the prayers of his people and the reception of his blessings, and having therefore enjoined habitual prayer as an indispensable condition of prosperity in the Divine life, they, in the devout conviction that by obeying the Lord's direction they would surely secure his favour, came together to entreat the fulfillment of his promises. They came together, not to go through a form, not to repeat set words, however excellent or even scriptural, but to pray, to call upon God as did the perishing mariners who were carrying Jonah to Tarshish, or as Peter did when he began to sink beneath the waves of Galilee. Immediate, pressing wants were before their minds, wants which no earthly power could meet; and they came to God with a feeling of entire dependence upon his power and grace. They cried aloud with fervour and constancy.

And they were answered with promptness and celerity never surpassed in the history of the Church. The instances were not rare in which persons under conviction of sin would have their condition spread out before God, and his grace implored in their behalf; and the next information which reached the Meeting would be that these very persons had passed from darkness to light, and were rejoicing in the assurance of forgiveness through the blood of Christ. At other times, prayer would be offered in behalf of souls far away, quite beyond the possibility of any direct efforts for them being put forth by those who presented their names; and it would be found afterwards, that just when God's people were praying, he was exerting his mighty power, even that power by which he raised our Lord Jesus Christ from the grave. "And it shall come to pass that before they call, I will answer; and while they are yet speaking I will hear." It was impossible not to notice these direct and speedy answers to prayer. They were thankfully acknowledged, and made the basis of renewed and earnest supplication for still greater blessings.

There was, therefore, a deep conviction that there is power in prayer, that it takes hold of the Almighty arm, that the connection between asking and receiving is as fixed and invariable as between any cause and its effect in the natural world. The hand of the Lord could operate any where and under all circumstances—just as well in a foreign land or in mid-ocean, as at home, where every means of instruction and appeal existed in profusion. Nothing was too hard for him. No case exceeded his power. No circumstances could exclude his gracious influence.

Encouraged by such unusual and striking manifestations of the Divine presence and faithfulness, men prayed with an ardour, a boldness, an urgency not often seen. Faith became more simple and mighty, in proportion to its simplicity. Cutting loose from an arm of flesh, it rested with full assurance upon the tried and sure word of God, and, as in the case of Abraham, hoped even against hope.

This has been decidedly the most distinguishing and

characteristic of all the features which marked the Word of Grace of the present year. It began in prayer, and it was carried on by prayer. Wherever the reviving and awakening influence of the Divine Spirit was enjoyed, almost invariably it was preceded by the assembling together of the people of God to pray. The Word of God was honoured, the various collateral agencies of the Church were recognized, the movements of Providence held a distinct and prominent place, but far above all other means towered this one of fervent, believing supplication. God was on the throne, and his people in the dust. Penetrated with a deep sense of unworthiness and helplessness, they took hold of the Divine covenant and promise, and pleaded them with an importunity like that of the Syro-Phenician woman, or of her who, by her continual coming, wrung even from an unjust judge the recognition of her rights.

God heard his own elect when they thus cried unto him. He turned their captivity. He did great things for them whereof they were glad. He poured out blessings even beyond their expectations. They could well address him in the Psalmist's words: "O thou that hearest prayer!"

V. The duty assigned to the writer of this Volume was simply that of narrator. His endeavour has been to weave together the chief facts which make up the history of the Noon Prayer Meeting, with such explanations as seemed necessary to show the connection of events, and put the distant reader on a level with those in the immediate vicinity of the place where God made this gracious development of his power and wisdom. It was no part of his purpose to sit in judgment upon the work itself or any of its details, or to furnish an exhaustive analysis of its principles and its lessons. But having ventured in this closing chapter to specify some of the more marked features of the history he has recorded, he is unwilling to conclude the Book without at least a caution on two points which seem to him of no small importance.

1. The first one of these is presented in the following brief extract from some remarks made in the Consistory building a month or two ago, by an intelligent gentleman from the interior of this state: "He considered that the great power of the Church for the conversion of souls now consisted in that union prayer meeting and the union Sunday school." Were this but one person's opinion, the matter would be scarcely worthy of notice. But there is reason to fear that many, carried away by the impulses of the hour, share in the same extravagant sentiment.

Beholding remarkable results following almost at once from the gathering of Christians of different names for prayer, and comparing this with the protracted periods during which the simple preaching of the word not unfrequently seems to be almost without effect, they leap to the conclusion that the latter is a worn out and obsolete instrumentality, and the union prayer meeting the chief means for bringing the latter-day glory.

To name this preposterous notion to a sober-minded man is to secure its condemnation. The ministry of the word and ordinances is and ever has been, and, we need not scruple to say, ever will be, the grand means of conviction, conversion and sanctification—all other agencies whatsoever being subordinate and accessory. To teach otherwise is to impeach the wisdom of Him who appointed this agency, and who has perpetuated it through all the ages of time down to our own day. To it He has given the commission, the promise, the authority and the blessing. More than once have men, fired with a zeal without knowledge, conceived the plan of a shorter road to great results, but they have always had to come back to the foolishness of preaching—the foolishness of God here as elsewhere being wiser than men. So will it surely be now, if the sentiment we are opposing, should succeed in gaining even a temporary foothold. But the misfortune is that while men are practically discovering the fallacy of the notion, great dishonour will be done to God, and great harm to the souls of men.

Fervent exhortation and conversational appeals are of inestimable value in supplementing and carrying out the instruction of the pulpit, but they cannot take its place. They lack the tone of authority, the systematic presentation of truth, the power to illuminate the understanding which the pulpit, honestly managed, always possesses. The usefulness of the union prayer meeting presupposes previous indoctrination of men by the ministry. Take away that groundwork for its exercises, and although feeling may be excited even to a violent pitch, it will be the rapid blaze of stubble leaving the field "burnt over" and hopeless, whereas the excitement which is based upon the truth, will last as long as the material upon which it rests.

2. The other error is the exaggerated importance attached to the exercises, and especially the prayer offered, in the Consistory building. Good people from all the parts of the country and even from the other side of the ocean, send requests for prayers to this Meeting, as if they supposed there was some

hidden efficacy, some mysterious power in the place or the persons occupying it, by virtue of which prayers offered there ascended directly and necessarily to the exalted Mediator, and were by Him so pleaded before the eternal Father as to secure a certain and immediate answer. Sometimes persons otherwise intelligent and pious, have been known to say that they "have great faith in the Fulton street Meeting"—thus degrading the object of faith from the word and promises of the Most High down to a mere company of fellow worms, themselves every day and every hour in need of the Divine compassion.

Here again to name the error is to condemn it. It is not to be denied that a sacred and tender interest attaches to the Consistory building, where the first Noon Prayer Meeting began. Doubtless, that spot has been the birth-place of more serious and saving impressions during the past year than any other in this land or elsewhere. Hallowed memories will endear it to the hearts of the people of God for generations to come. But all this is no excuse for giving to it the honour which is due to God alone. And if there be in the whole category of human events one thing which is calculated to strip it of its prestige, to cause ICHABOD to be written upon its walls and to render it offensive and abominable, it is this of regarding it with superstitious reverence, and tying down the glorious and adorable sovereignty of omnipotent grace to its prayers and intercessions, every one of which, however fervent and spiritual, yet needs to be sprinkled with atoning blood, before it can enter with the least acceptance into the presence of the Most High.

God is a jealous God, and his glory will he not give another. The attempt has often been made in the history of the Church to rob him of his honour under various plausible pretences, some of them exhibiting a remarkable counterfeit of gratitude and piety, but in the end his outraged dignity has avenged itself to the confusion and dismay of those who rashly invaded the crown rights of Zion's great King. And as the Lord has done before, so He can and He will do, now and hereafter.

But the Author, while compelled by a sense of duty, not to be satisfied in any other way, to express these views, yet hopes better things and things which accompany salvation, although he thus speaks. He hopes that God in his mercy will give grace to the brethren who assemble daily in the old spot, to guard carefully their own hearts; that he will clothe them with humility as with a garment; that he will imbue them more and more with a sense of their entire dependence, and inspire them with the mind of those glorified saints in heaven, who, exalted as they are, yet cast their crowns at the feet of the Lamb. With such a spirit dominant in all hearts, with penitence and humility going hand in hand with faith and zeal, with the maintenance of a zealous regard for the Divine honour, there will be reason to look for a continuance, and even an increase of the blessings hitherto vouchsafed. The House of Prayer shall be a House of Mercy, a genuine Bethesda to innumerable souls, and the fervour of petition shall be rivalled by the fervour of thanksgiving for what God has done and is doing in the unsearchable riches of his grace.

NOW UNTO THE KING, ETERNAL, IMMORTAL,
INVISIBLE, THE ONLY WISE GOD,
BE HONOUR AND GLORY FOR EVER AND EVER. AMEN.

CPSIA information can be obtained
at www.ICGtesting.com
Printed in the USA
BVHW031448250121
598582BV00004B/284